INDEPENDENTS FOR EAST HERTS

Jim Thornton

INDEPENDENTS FOR EAST HERTS
Copyright © Jim Thornton 2010

All Rights Reserved

British Library Cataloguing in Publication Data

A catalogue record for this book is available from the British Library

ISBN 978 0 9532398 3 2

First Published 2010 by
Church Home Group Resources Ltd
25 Castle Street, Hertford SG14 1HH

T: +44 (0) 1992 515576
F: +44 (0) 1992 509625
E: info@CHGRL.org

Printed in Great Britain by
www.direct-pod.com

INDEPENDENTS
FOR EAST HERTS

CONTENTS

Introduction   7

1   The Art of the Possible   9
2   Getting Started in Politics   13
3   The Local Government Hierarchy   15
4   Planning is not Political   19
5   Fighting an Election   23
6   Getting out the Vote   27
7   Losing an Election   29
8   Getting Selected as a Candidate   33
9   Finding Candidates   37
10   Campaigning on Local Issues   41
11   Writing Your Manifesto   45
12   Election Administration   51
13   The Count   57
14   The Newly Elected Councillor   61
15   How Much Time does it Take?   65
16   Officers and Members   69
17   Working as a Group   73
18   The Media   77
19   Scrutiny   81
20   Backbenchers have None of the Fun   85
21   Starting your own Party   87
22   The Benefit of Researchers   93
23   Fighting as an Independent   97

24	Financing Your Campaign		101
25	The Independent Network		103
26	Can Independents be Effective?		105
	Appendix 1	The Bell Principles	109
	Appendix 2	Laura's Diary	111
	Appendix 3	Livia's Diary	143
	Appendix 4	James's Diary	169
	Appendix 5	Postscript	179

Have you ever thought you could do a better job than our elected politicians?

Have you ever wondered how you could get elected?

Have you ever been put off doing anything about this, because you have no idea how to begin, and would not have a clue what to do if you actually did get elected?

This book will tell you how to go about getting elected, what happens next, and why you are unlikely to be able to change the world over night. However, a motto of local politicians is that Mountains can always be Climbed One Step at a Time.

Although the examples I write about come from East Herts, a District Council area in the home counties just north of London, I know from talking to colleagues around the country that the issues we face are pretty much the same everywhere.

I was trained by the Conservative Party, but have come to see the merits of being an Independent Councillor in local government. I think there is also a good argument for a group of Independents in the House of Commons, doing the excellent work that the cross-benchers do in the Lords.

"But how can I get involved in real live politics?" you ask.

Let me tell you a story ......

1
The Art of the Possible

The note was passed to me along the row, and I looked to see who had written it. The Council Chamber was packed full of Conservative Councillors, almost a full house for this important Group Meeting. Mike was looking straight at me, so it must be his note. *"Are you going to propose a vote of no confidence in the Leader?"*

I thought hard. We had won the first vote, but I did not think we would win this one, so this was the defining moment: go down gloriously, or live to fight another day?

Mike wrote for the Financial Times, among other things, and was bright and ambitious. He had been working alongside the Back Bench Committee during the scandal that was developing.

Next to me was Duncan, larger than life, an excellent elected Councillor on Town, District and County Councils, a finger in every pie. He had a colourful past, doing property work with the person *Private Eye* calls 'Changi Jim' Slater, back in the golden days of the seventies and eighties. He loved to stir things up, and I really enjoyed working with him. When I was allowed to set up the Back Bench Committee I made it a condition that we had a new chairman each year. Duncan succeeded me, but enjoyed it so much we could not get him to hand over to anyone else. I was now the Secretary and did the administration.

Somebody was droning on, and now Duncan was prodding me: *"What are we going to do?"* he hissed.

The Leader of the Council was in the chair, and his Cabinet of Portfolio Holders sat close to him to protect him from the mob. We were the mob, the ordinary elected Councillors, the Back Benchers, the ones who had no specific job to do and were expected to support the Party Leadership, right or wrong.

The *Hertfordshire Mercury* had headlined their front page with "WE'VE WON!" on 2 December 2005. They had spent £30,000 of their own money to get the High Court to lift large parts of an injunction from the Council to stop the publication of a Report.

Although the Report and investigation had cost the tax-payer £120,000, we as ordinary Councillors were not allowed to read it. Now we could, thanks to the *Mercury*. Bullying, sexual harassment, in-fighting between officers, wasted money, it was all there in the released Report.

The previous weekend I had met at my house with Duncan and Jim, the elder statesman of the Conservative Group. We wanted to find a face-saving way for the Leader to resign. Jim had read chemistry at Oxford, had probably the best brain on the Council, and was the only Councillor who read all the Council Papers.

We had agreed a proposal, and Jim reluctantly agreed to phone the Leader. Jim told me it was one of the hardest phone calls of his life, but he told me we had a deal.

But when we came to the meeting, it was clear we did not have a deal. The Leader refused to leave the Council Chamber to allow us to have a discussion without him. I had no alternative but to propose a motion that the Leader leave the meeting. We won by 21 votes to about 14, and that was the turning point. The Leader knew that the game was up, and with bad grace he left the room, leaving his Cabinet to defend him.

The Report had found evidence to support union claims of a 'culture of bullying, blame and fear', and it was clear that the Leader had not been straight with his Party, the Councillors or the media. However, political parties defend their own, unless it is incest or paedophilia, and even then there is a hesitation. The unforgivable sin is disloyalty, and for that it is outer darkness and no Christmas Card from the MP.

The choice was: either make him go now, or ask him to stand for re-election in a few months time in March 2006. The Leader had stitched up the Constitution so we could not get rid of him until May 2007. While I thought he had handled the whole thing appallingly and if he had any sense of honour or shame he should have resigned, in politics you have to deal with the art of the possible.

I chose the route I thought we could win, and proposed the re-election option. And this is one of the hardest lessons in politics: *you sometimes have to choose between winning a bit or losing the lot.* While losing may sometimes be morally satisfactory, your voters elected you to win benefits for them, not lose them on issues of personal principle.

We did win the vote to make him stand for re-election, but a month later the County Conservative Party forced him to resign anyway. The tragedy was that a majority of my colleagues refused to apologise to the electorate for what had happened. They elected the Deputy Leader as Leader, and carried on with the same team, and business as usual.

I was not going to defend such behaviour to the voters. I decided I would stand at the next election in 2007 as an Independent. I made the Conservatives throw me out, rather than make it easy by resigning, so members would know important issues of principle were involved. I appealed to David Cameron, but his office said it was a local issue, and he could not get involved.

I was on my own with no party organisation to support me. How easy would it be, on my own, as an Independent?

How does anyone get started in politics from scratch?

2
Getting Started

My first job came through political action. I enjoyed student life at Manchester, so stayed on for another year to do a Masters in the Economics and Statistics of Town Planning. It was a wonderful summer, and for my research I had to cycle round selected areas of Leeds, Sheffield and Bradford knocking on people's doors and asking if they still had an outside privy. As that year came to an end, I had to think about getting a job in the real world.

I was a member of the Liberals, not a very active one, but I was asked to help with an anti-apartheid demonstration by applying to civil engineering companies for a job in South Africa and making a protest to the interviewing team. We were interviewed two at a time, and in my case it was an old-time Afrikaner from Roberts Construction named Vaughan. "When you come to South Africa," he told us in his thick yarpie accent, "you will realise that the military has left its mark on the population, so we expect you to get your hair cut."

My student colleague told him we had no intention of working in South Africa, or getting our hair cut, and were appalled at what was going on. I made similar noises, and Vaughan rolled his eyes, and said: "We can give you a job in Zambia if you like."

I sat up. I had done my gap year in Kenya, and once Africa gets in your blood, it is impossible to get rid of it. "Would you really get me through my civils in Zambia?" I asked.

"Sure," he said.

So I soon found myself in a room at the YMCA in Kitwe as a Junior Engineer on the Copperbelt, trying to write up my MA dissertation in the evenings.

It was impossible to get involved in any politics in Zambia. The fear of all expatriates was being 'PI'd', or being declared a 'Prohibited Immigrant' and expelled from the country.

The nearest I came to this was when I played the National Anthem in the wrong key. The music notation is actually included in the Act of Parliament, and it is a serious offence to mess with it. One expat was PI'd for recording it on a twin track tape, and when he pushed the button with everybody standing to attention, it was the wrong track and they got the Tijuana Brass instead.

I think it was a Remembrance Day service, and they suddenly turned to me and said the band had cold feet about the National Anthem, so would I play it instead. I can sight read most things, but cannot play by ear or memory. It was either the key of C or the key of G, and I could not remember which. I chose the wrong one, and the sight of the Mayor and Councillors trying to get top Gs was worth seeing.

My next posting was Bahrain, where again it was almost impossible to get involved in politics. This is not entirely true, as anyone who does business in the Gulf knows how important it is to have the right political connections. Bahrain has a large Shia population, which created difficulties for the Sunni rulers. The Chief of Police learned his trade with the Mau-Mau in Kenya, and you did not ask questions about human rights.

Two of our three children were born in Bahrain, but after six years we returned as a family to the UK and settled in Hertford. My wife had been on the staff of All Souls, Langham Place, and after a service I had asked Michael Allison MP how he advised getting started in politics. "Get stuck in with your local party, and get on the Ward Committee," was his advice. So I did.

3
The Local Government Hierarchy

I had a look round Hertford, where we had come to live. We chose Hertford for its good train links to central London, and in this part of the commuter belt, the Conservatives dominated the landscape. If politics is the art of getting things done, I reasoned, then joining any other party would be masochism.

When I expressed an interest, I was welcomed and eventually asked to join a Ward Committee. And so began years of cheese and wine, strawberry teas and often boring evening committee meetings.

We tried to do our own share of hosting events, but Viv did not really share my interest in politics. On one occasion she reluctantly agreed to let the politicians in for a celebration, and minutes before they started to arrive she found a large rat from the barn next door sitting in the middle of the lounge floor. Our two boys were pushed into the room with a cricket bat, and not allowed out until it had been dealt with. Rats in the lounge was rather how she felt about politics and politicians.

The basic building block of local politics is the **Ward**, the area in which you live and for which you elect representatives. You can look up electoral boundaries on www.election-maps.co.uk which is a website run by Ordnance Survey. The curious thing is that a Ward as a unit of government is a virtual reality, as it has no visible infrastructure or organisation.

If you want to find out more about your Ward, the best thing to do is contact the local Electoral Registration Office and buy the

Electoral Register. You will find www.aboutmyvote.com very helpful. This will cost about £25 per Ward and they can email you an electronic copy.

From this you can see every house in the Ward that has a voter living in it. It is possible to have your name removed from public view and still vote, so the list you get will probably be the edited Register, and will not list every voter. If you are running as a candidate you can get a free copy of the full Electoral Register, but you may want to do some analysis before you decide to declare as a candidate, so you will have no choice but to buy the edited version.

In those days of the early eighties, each Ward had its own Conservative Party committee, and these committees reported to the **Area** Committee. The Labour Party had a similar organisation.

In the case of Hertford, there are four Wards, but the Conservative Hertford Area included some of the rural wards around the town as well. The Ward we lived in elected four councillors to the Town Council, three to East Herts District Council, and with an adjoining Ward, one Councillor to Hertfordshire County Council.

Many voters have no idea what each Council does, and most do not even know which Ward they live in.

Parish and Town Councils

Hertford Town Council is legally a **Parish Council**, and its main remit is Cemeteries and Allotments. At that time in the mid-eighties the whole show was pretty much run single-handedly by the indomitable Ann Kirby. Now it has a staff of goodness knows how many, and they organise band concerts and trade fairs in the Castle Grounds, and try and do what they can to support the economic life of the town.

There is a great deal of history to the Town Council, and you either like tradition and robes and funny hats, or you do not. The Town Council keeps the traditions going.

There is also an interesting anomaly in that a Parish Council can still raise a Precept for as much money as it wants. So Hertford Town Council could technically have asked for £100m to invest in Iceland, and the tax payers would have had to cough up.

I have argued to some of my colleagues that the only way to get a better calibre of Parish Councillor is to push more power down to the Parish Councils. This is not thought to be a good idea, as there is a fear of what some village with rogue Councillors might get up to. Jeremy Clarkson once argued the case for Parish Councils in his column in *The Times*, but it comes down to how many politicians per head you believe the country needs for good governance, and whether they should be paid or voluntary.

District and County Councils

The **District Council** does an extraordinary number of things, but the really important things like Education and Social Services are done by the **County Council**.

The main problem is remembering who collects the rubbish and who cuts the grass, the two major problems in East Herts.

So Town or Parish Councillors are at the bottom of the hierarchy, but this is a good training ground. District Councillors have more real power and a huge variety of small things to look after, but the tough job is on the County Council which has a Budget of £1.2 billion.

The problem was that once the Ward Committee had worked hard to get the Councillors elected, with honourable exceptions you rarely saw your Councillors again until the next election. The Ward Committee had no control over the way the Councillors voted, and so policy discussions were generally a complete waste of time.

I expected to be able to influence local government policy by joining the Ward Committee, but I found this was not the way it worked. This is why it is so hard to recruit committee members. I could not even do anything about Tesco's planning application, apart from rant at the rest of the Committee.

But then *planning is not political*. If you want to stand for election to stop your neighbour's house extension, then you are in for a shock. Planning is a quasi-judicial function of the Council.

4
Planning is not Political

Anybody able to read a set of plans would have looked at the Leisure Centre planning application and said: "This looks like a gravel pit with some tennis courts in it". The only problem was that this was a flat site in the green belt, and adjoining an area of suburban housing, and it was not really clear why the developer felt it was necessary to sink everything so deeply into the ground.

The Council granted planning permission, the lorries rolled in, the hole was dug and the gravel removed, and then the developer left it to rot. To this day, no Leisure Centre has been built, and for years the local residents were disturbed by motor cycles and kids having a great time.

What made me so angry was that I felt it was such an obvious scam that the Council Officers should have stopped it. There were worse allegations, but whatever the truth, I wanted to use this as a campaign issue.

I was very firmly told that *Planning is not Political*. The Planning Committee has a quasi-judicial role, and politics must not be allowed to influence decisions.

I admire Councillors who sit on Planning Committees up and down the country. They do an immense amount of hard work, give a lot of time, risk being surcharged if they get it wrong, and get little thanks from the electorate who live next door to the developments they approve. Being in the property industry, I kept well away from the Planning Committee.

One complaint is that in the old days, a Ward Councillor expected to be able to act as an advocate for a voter who was making an application, or for one who was objecting. Today you have to be very careful that what you say or do does not bring a complaint to the **Standards Board**.

While it is important that high standards are maintained, for many Councillors a complaint to the Standards Board can be devastating. For those of us in business, threats of legal action are part and parcel of a day's work, but for somebody who does not work in the business world, the process of the complaint can damage their health.

It is not unknown for a party to make a trumped up complaint to the Standards Board as a way of intimidating an opponent, and this has contributed to the weakening of the links between Ward Councillor and voter.

Various ideas have been proposed: do you let the Parish Council decide Planning Applications? Or rather, refuse every application put to it? Or do you give the power to a remote Council covering a large area, where Councillors who live in completely different surroundings dare to impose outrageous things on you and your neighbours?

On balance it is probably better if councillors from miles away can be blamed for unpopular decisions. If it is to be a quasi-judicial process, then I would want a decision to be made impartially, based on the agreed Local Plan. If I came up before a local court, and found the magistrate was my next door neighbour, I would object and ask for somebody I did not know. In the same way, it is better if the local Councillors can act as advocates on planning decisions, but the decision should be made by others.

This is infuriating to many people as they feel they are being denied an opportunity to be heard. One problem is the sheer volume of applications, and one solution that has been proposed is to allow the Parish Council to *approve* planning applications but not refuse them. Those refused permission go up to the next level of government.

If you want to be a Councillor in order to stop any more building in your street, then forget it – this is not the way the system works.

But if you have higher ambitions, and decide to become a candidate, then you have to think about how you are going to fight your election campaign.

5
Fighting an Election

I arrived back from the Gulf in time to help with the 1983 General Election. I was asked to do some Telling at the Polling Station in Hertingfordbury, a small picturesque village on the outskirts of Hertford.

The Polling Station was in the local Cricket Pavilion, and I was doing a couple of hours from five o'clock. As a Teller you are not allowed inside the Polling Station, so you sit on a chair outside, wearing your rosette, and you record the Electoral Number of everybody who comes to vote (and who agrees to give it you).

The sky was blue, not a cloud to be seen, the grass of the cricket pitch had been freshly mown, and at six o'clock a butler in morning dress appeared from the White Horse Hotel with three pints of cold beer on a silver salver for the two clerks and me. Oh to be in England! This is how to do politics I thought, what a wonderful world.

But what is the point of Telling, and how does it help win an election?

Here is a simple guide to fighting a traditional election:

- Knock on every door and ask each voter how they intend to vote (where many people live in a household, they are unlikely to all be opening the door to you at once). This is called **canvassing**.

- Identify who in the household is going to vote for your party, and who is therefore a 'Supporter'

- Have a **Teller** at every Polling Station for every hour it is open (probably 7am to 10pm)

- Record on a Voting Slip the Polling Number of every voter who comes to vote

- Get these Voting Slips to the **Committee Room** in the Ward every hour (usually a lad on a bicycle collects them from the tellers)

- The volunteers in the Committee Room (somebody's front room or garage) ticks off your Supporters who have voted

- By 5pm you can produce a list of Supporters in the Ward who have not yet voted

- You divide this list into geographical areas and give volunteers a list of people to **'Knock Up'**

- This means knocking on their door or telephoning them and asking them to get out and vote

- The game is won by the Party that gets the largest number of their Supporters to the Polling Station

Of course, this has all been messed up now by Postal Votes, the lack of volunteers, and the standard response on the doorstep when you ask the voter who they are going to vote for: *"None of your business, mate."*

Did it work? Yes, it did, and in particular because it was a good way of involving a lot of people in a team effort, for a worthwhile cause, for a limited period of time. That was in the days before most normal people became disillusioned with politicians and politics generally.

But it is a truism that whoever persuades the greatest number of their potential Supporters to overcome their apathy, wins the election.

6
Getting out the Vote

I remember once taking my Knocking Up list and hiding behind a hedge for an hour ....

When I had attended enough Ward Committee Meetings, I was asked to stand for the Town Council in Sele, a solid Labour seat. The only time the Conservatives had won a seat there was when a long-serving highly regarded Councillor called Bob Perrett retired. The Conservatives found a young man called Perry and put him up, hoping enough people would be confused and vote for him. There were enough, and he got elected. Apparently, it was the best thing that could have happened to him, and revolutionised his life.

But Sele was gradually being gentrified. The young people who had originally moved onto the estate when it was built were prospering. They had built a good community, which began to grow away from traditional Labour values. The Liberal Democrats saw an opportunity.

Bridget and Paul Fox had recently moved to Hertford, and had bolstered the Liberal Party, as it then was. Bridget is now Deputy Leader of Islington and a Prospective Parliamentary Candidate, but she informed me that she would be standing against me in Sele. It would therefore be a three-way split which I thought would make it impossible for the Conservatives to win.

We started off on our traditional campaign, and each week I would compare notes with Bridget and Paul, her campaign manager. They used to sit behind us in St Andrews Church, so it was easy to keep in touch. I became increasingly concerned, as my canvass returns supported theirs – it was going to be a three way split, with any of the three as potential winners. I was worried because my work commitments at that time would make it impossible for me to be an effective Councillor.

Ten days before the election, Paul whispered across the pew that he thought I was slightly ahead. In the Anglican Church in the middle of the service, we have 'the Peace', when we shake hands with each other. When it came to this point, I turned round to Bridget and said: "The Peace of the Lord be with you – and I hope you win, because I don't have time to be an effective Councillor."

The next day, they delivered a letter to all the Conservative pledges saying that Jim Thornton had wished the Liberal Candidate success as he did not have time to be a Councillor. I thought this was turning into a really fun election, but the Party Hierarchy was not impressed, and they demanded and got an apology from the Chairman of the Liberals in Hertford, who was also a member of St Andrews. We generally had candidates from all the parties in the Church for each local election.

When it came to Election Day, I was seriously worried. I was given a list of twenty names to go and knock up, but I hid behind a bush for an hour pretending I was out knocking on doors. I lost by twelve votes.

Most knocking up is now done by telephone, but the problem today is identifying who your core supporters are, and the old tried and tested methods are no longer quite as reliable.

If you are an Independent, how do you identify your supporters? How do you get them out to vote for you? Before you start worrying about this, you need to face up to the possibility that you *might not win*, and you need to be sure you can cope with the disappointment of losing.

7
Losing an Election

Before you start thinking seriously about standing for election, you <u>must</u> prepare yourself psychologically for losing.

Most of the people I ask to stand for election assume they will win, and however hard I try, they are devastated when they lose. Mind you, one election when I assured them and promised them they would not win, they all did. None of them attended the count, and I had to drive around at 4am leaving apologetic notes at their homes.

Sally lived in a working farm on the outskirts of Hertford, and we knew she would be a good candidate. We persuaded her to stand for the District Council in Bengeo. She lost, and this had convinced her never to stand again, as she found it humiliating.

She had done well in a difficult fight, and when there was a sudden by-election, we had a major job persuading her to go through the agony again. An election is hard work for a candidate who wants to win, and when you do the hard work and still lose, this is devastating.

We finally managed to get Sally on the ballot paper. We all worked really hard, and I remember the count particularly keenly, as I was the one who had twisted her arm and I felt personally responsible for the result. She lost again, and I was convinced we would never ever persuade her to go through the humiliation of another election. It is hard not to take it personally – you feel that the voters have rejected <u>you</u>, not your party.

So when it came to the next election in 2003, I am not sure now how we managed to get Sally to stand for a third time, but I remember it was a major effort. This time she won, and now she is a Cabinet Member on Hertfordshire County Council.

How can you psych yourself up to accept that you did not win?

Here are three ideas:

- **In an election, at least one person has to lose:** it is an essential part of a lively and viable democracy that there should be a choice of candidates.

  In Africa some tried to argue to me that a one-party state is the 'African Way', where decisions are made under the big tree and only when consensus is reached. However, there were plenty of other African friends who recognised the need to hold politicians to account, and free and fair elections are probably the least worst option.

  To have an election, you have to have at least two candidates, and one will have to lose. Convince yourself that you are doing an honourable job by providing a choice, and losers are an essential part of a just and democratic society.

- **Elections are great fun:** spend a few weeks having a great time.

- **Get to know the neighbours:** as a candidate, you have the right to knock on anybody's door, speak to them in the street, write to them, or shout at them through a loud-hailer. When you are wearing a rosette, people know it is about an election and you are a candidate.

If you knock on somebody's door without your rosette, they will treat you with suspicion – are you a Jehovah's Witness, a Double-Glazing Salesman, or what?

But if you are a candidate in a forthcoming election, people want to talk to you, and you can have a great few weeks chatting to the neighbours you do not know, and making new friends and acquaintances in your community.

Before you can lose an election, you have to fight one, and before you can fight an election, you need to be a candidate. So how do you become a candidate?

8
Getting Selected as a Candidate

I had a call from the Area Chairman: would I be willing to stand for election to the County Council in 1997? The Hertford St Andrews Division was then held by a Labour Councillor, Sir Norman Lindop, former Vice-Chancellor of the University of Hertfordshire and Chairman of the County Council.

How do you get selected as a party candidate? It is down to the Ward Committee initially, but the Constituency Committee will probably have the final say by retaining the right to approve all candidates.

Whether or not the Party system is the best way to do politics, the problem is that the candidates we get to vote for are selected by a very small number of people, some of whom would be considered complete fanatics or fruitcakes by normal voters.

The problem of Party is really the problem of how you democratise the Party, control the nutcases, stop Buggins's turn, and open the doors as wide as possible to the greatest number of potential candidates.

The Party would say that the problem is: *'how can we be sure they are one of us?'*

In the eighties we would interview volunteers who wanted to be candidates for the Town and District Councils. The Party Members would generally be willing to let the Ward Committee get on with it, as they knew that they had the opportunity each

33

year to elect the Ward Committee. As the membership has shrunk, so have the volunteers to be on a Ward Committee, and so have the numbers of people wanting to be candidates. In recent years, I think the only selection committees we had were for the County Council seat.

It was therefore a sign of the times in 1997 that the Area Chairman was reduced to phoning round trying to find somebody who was even willing to stand for the County.

Stay or Go?

In 1995 there had been a complete rout following the rise of New Labour. In the 1995 election all the old guard were thrown out, and only Peter Ruffles, a local teacher, remained as the one Conservative on the District and the one Conservative on the Town Council.

Ruffles MBE is a local institution, who knows everybody in Hertford and taught most of them. Since 1995, most of my friends had stopped supporting the Conservative Party, and in 1997 I had to decide what I would do. Would I stay or would I join Labour or the Liberal Democrats or the Greens?

For a number of reasons I felt that the Conservatives were really where I belonged; there were lots of faults, but I believed I would stand a better chance in the long term of working for a better world as a wet Tory than as a dry Lib Dem. I therefore agreed to stand for the County, believing that if I did this, then I would be owed (a) a safe seat for the District or Town at the next election and (b) a bigger voice on the Party committees. I lost to Sir Norman, but I reduced his majority.

Area Chairman

And so it was that in the February before the 1999 May elections, the old guard came to me and asked me to take over as Area Chairman. They had few candidates for the election, and the whole organisation had collapsed. I had little time, and although I managed to get the ten candidates needed for the District Council, I managed to find less than half the sixteen candidates needed for the Town Council.

I was allowed to draft the manifesto and decide what we campaigned on. I had consciously tried to avoid spin and knocking copy, and to be fair to all points of view, but the election material I produced was not very good, and we were very short of workers on the ground.

However, we worked hard and the surprising result was that this time instead of just Peter Ruffles being elected, I was elected as well - by a majority of 40 votes. Needless to say I had put myself in the seat most likely to be won, but the Conservatives had gone from two Hertford seats to three Hertford seats, out of a total of twenty-six. Peter and I were together on East Herts District Council, and Peter still had to battle it out on his own in the Hertford Town Council.

I have to admit that I had not expected how hard it had been to find candidates.

9
Finding Candidates

If you are keen to stand as a candidate, and are willing to wear a party label, then you will probably have no difficulty in finding a Ward in which to stand for the lower levels of local government. They are unlikely to give you a winnable seat first time round, but all the parties are desperate for good candidates.

For the 2003 election, Peter and I started to try and find candidates well before Christmas 2002, and we worked through a long list of around 90 names. We decided to forget about choosing Conservative party members (they were all very elderly anyway) and we would go out into the highways and byways and invite people of good will who did not mind the stigma of being a Conservative.

We had to work very hard, and many people either said 'no' or 'next time'. Nominations closed on Tuesday 1 April, and on the Saturday before, three of the candidates dropped out, giving me a difficult weekend. On the Monday night I had a candidate for every seat bar two, all proposed and seconded and signed up.

In two wards, Bengeo and Sele, we were one short on the Town Council list. Bengeo up until eight years ago was always a Conservative ward, and was one of the two Hertford wards that still had a Conservative Ward Committee. None of the committee would stand, and in desperation Peter and I went back through our lists: I was determined we would put up a full list in Bengeo to demonstrate we were serious contenders.

The only possible candidate was a 21 year old from an interesting family background, whom Peter believed would agree to be a candidate. When Peter had suggested him several months previously, I had refused to consider him.

However, being desperate, at 8pm I went to his house willing to have anybody to complete the list. He was not there, and I was partly relieved; I was getting into my car resigned to being two short, when his mother arrived and told me he was working in the White Horse at Hertingfordbury as a barman. She had just returned from delivering Labour Party leaflets.

I drove round to the pub, bought a pint, and asked him if he had ever thought of being a Councillor? At 8.50pm he signed the forms, I took his photo against the bar wall for his election leaflet, and I went round to two committee members who proposed and seconded him. The forms were accepted by the Council just before the close of nominations at noon.

The final list of candidates showed we were a very mixed bunch.

There were several who had stood before, but I still had to arm-twist them to stand again for the honour of the Party; it really does hurt to be rejected by the electorate.

One or two were really keen, and one of these was the 27 year old chairman of the Hertford Skate Park Group.

A Skatepark for Hertford

As chairman of Forum West I had been petitioned by 60 teenagers for a skatepark in Hertford. I was still new and green, and thought this would be easy.

It had been eighteen months of hard work pushing a rock uphill, but the Labour run Town Council made a tactical mistake by refusing to agree to pay for the maintenance: it therefore became a political issue, because without Town Council support the District would not provide the land and the capital funding.

This was not a wise move, as it became 'vote Conservative for a skateboard park'. The Labour Party suddenly realised their mistake, and gave a last minute election pledge to support the park, but by then it was too late and we had got our message across.

We had organised a major consultation with 100 young people and from this put together seven teenagers/twenties as the Hertford Skate Park Group of which I became honorary treasurer.

At one meeting in frustration I half jokingly asked if any of the committee would like to stand for the Town Council to persuade them to take over the running of the park, and Matt the chairman agreed.

His fiancée was a politics graduate, and they came to the Conservative briefing for new candidates, and it was like taking someone to an evangelistic rally: I worried that someone would say something offensive (hang 'em and flog 'em, or ban single mums). But at the end of the meeting it was like a conversion – Matt was all fired up to get out and door knock, and said he had not realised how much the Council did, and how wonderful it all was and so on, and so on .....

Then there were the ones I had to really push: my hard-working secretary, Helle, for example. I promised her she would not get elected in the safe Labour ward in which she lived – there had been no Conservatives there for over twenty years.

The young managing director of the company in the office next door – I promised him he would not get elected, either. Others reluctantly agreed to stand on my assurance that there was no chance of them being elected, but they might enjoy an election.

In the end I had a diverse crew of 17 standing in 25 out of the 26 seats, and only two did not get elected to the seats for which they stood. One of whom was me.

Start as Early as You Can

But if you want to be a candidate in an election where you have a fight on your hands, then you need to prepare well in advance and get yourself known in your Ward.

You could:

- become a School Governor
- get involved with a Parent Teachers Association
- join the Neighbourhood Watch
- join a Residents Association
- volunteer to help with a local charity
- join a sports or special interest club committee

Single issue campaigns are also a great way of getting yourself known, and you are bound to have some local issues that get people excited.

10
Campaigning on Local Issues

In 1989 I had to tell my wife that I had lost everything in the property crash, and the Royal Bank of Scotland would probably repossess the house and make us homeless.

The week before my companies went into administration, we had an urgent call from the BBC asking if they could film a morning service for BBC1 from our home, and interview me about faith in business.

The children thought it was a joke, but when the BBC lorries parked outside the house and the cameras appeared, they realised it was for real. I told the presenter about the irony of the situation, and he told me he had gone bankrupt the previous year, and there actually was life after financial disaster.

We started researching, and found out that we, as a family, would be statutorily homeless, and so the local Council would have to re-house us. What we also discovered was that there was no provision at that time for young people aged 18-25, and there was quite a hidden problem in the area, with young people thrown out of home sleeping on friend's floors.

I shall always be grateful to the Royal Bank of Scotland that when I had managed to repay the loan, they waived the interest and did not make us homeless. So partly in gratitude we started to get involved with young homeless issues, and helped set up the **Hertford Young Homeless Group.**

Eventually the law changed, but during that time we met some very interesting people, both volunteers and young homeless. We started a Crash Pad in our home, but had to drop it when one of the young people tried to sell our son some drugs.

By this time I also had office staff working in the house, and one of my employees has never really recovered from the morning when one of the youngsters came down and asked for help with her septic belly-button. Some DIY piercing had gone a bit wrong.

Getting involved with a local volunteer organisation is a great way of getting an insight into how local politics works. We lobbied the local Councillors, and began to find out from them the limits of what they could do and why. We learned about raising funds for local projects, and were amazed when we received a cheque from the J Paul Getty Charitable Trust for the Green Dragon Vaults youth project.

Viv, my wife, got involved with the **Keep Sunday Special Campaign**, working with Trade Unions and local traders to try and preserve some weekend family life for those in the retail trade. Bowen Wells, our MP, was not convinced about the issue, and reluctantly agreed to 'try and call in for ten minutes' on the public meeting Viv organised.

On a cold February evening the Richard Hale school hall was almost full, and when Bowen did arrive, he realised he had totally miscalculated, stayed for the whole meeting, and was well and truly taken apart by some very articulate people. When it came to the vote in Parliament, he abstained.

This was my first introduction to the importance of people power, and the fact that if you get it right, you _can_ make a difference. It really helps to have a good cause, as Dr Richard Taylor found at Kidderminster when the threat to close the local hospital became the wave on which he rode into Parliament in 2001.

But is single issue politics the best way forward in a normal election? I am not convinced it is, but out of these experiences I did develop the idea that a possible way to use the popularity of single issues was to chose a list of four or five single issues to define the outlook of a group of candidates. We used this to great advantage in our campaign in 2003.

You will want to send round a leaflet to all the voters, telling them what you are standing for. Calling it a 'Manifesto' may sound a bit grand, as you do not have much space on a sheet of A4 which is probably all you can print to keep within the spending limit.

However, unless you tell the voters *something,* they can hardly be expected to vote for you.

11
Writing Your Manifesto

How do you tell people what you stand for?

At local level, you are generally relying on the brand image, such as Conservatives wanting to be tight with the money, Labour wanting to spend it, and Lib Dems being for those who want to have it and spend it and can't decide what they want. The problem is that there is no Conservative Policy on dog fouling of footpaths, or Lib Dem Policy on working hours for the Market Beadle.

When you are in opposition in local government, you have to overcome the national brand image, and give people a good reason to vote for *you*.

I decided for the 2003 Town and District elections that we would select four Projects that were needed in Hertford and make sure we got them done. These were:

- a skateboard park

- a cinema

- a charitable trust to enable the public to make tax efficient donations to small community projects, and

- affordable housing for teachers on the Mill Road site.

In the disastrous 1995 election the District Council became a hung council, with no party in an overall majority. This was hard work. East Herts Council covers one third of the County of Hertfordshire, and is mainly rural, but with five towns of which Hertford is the second largest.

Town and Country

Previously East Herts Council had been fairly solidly Conservative, and in 1999 when I was first elected, the Conservatives held 31 out of 50 seats, of which fifteen were in the rural areas. People would joke that in these villages a cow could get elected on a Conservative ticket, and uncontested elections are common.

Hertford had the only six Labour Councillors, plus two Liberal Democrats, and me and Peter as the only two Conservatives; there were no other Labour Councillors in the District, but a number of Liberal Democrats in Bishops Stortford and Ware.

With fifteen Councillors from the villages and sixteen from the Towns, the village councillors tended to dominate, as they had been around the longest. Because they do not have to fight elections (two were unopposed), they often lose touch with the political realities that those of us in the Towns have to face.

The village Councillors drafted the 2003 election manifesto for the District, and it made pretty ghastly reading. I refused to use it, and fortunately I was backed by the senior political agent for the party in Hertfordshire. The quality of production of the District leaflet was grim, and again I had to upset the hierarchy by insisting on a heavier quality paper in a brilliant white; again, I was backed by the Senior Political Agent, for which I was very grateful.

A Manifesto for Hertford

In Hertford we did not promise in the East Herts Council Manifesto to reduce the Council tax like the country cousins wanted us to do, but instead we promised (a) to benchmark our tax against the other nine Districts in the County and aim to keep in the lower half and (b) to benchmark our services provision as well and aim to be in the upper half for quality and cost efficiency.

We pushed our four Projects. I had described them in the local paper the previous year, so people knew these were serious projects being worked on, and not simply an election gimmick.

In the Town Council manifesto, we pointed out that our Town tax had increased by 123% over 8 years of Labour administration, and while we acknowledged that Labour had done some good things, we also pointed out that our tax was considerably above the tax per head in Bishops Stortford and Ware. We believed we could provide the same services for a cost closer to that in the other Towns.

One of the village councillors, who looked after the Finance portfolio on the District Council Executive, decided in an election year to cut the grant to the Citizens Advice Bureaux by £60,000; this was an absolute gift to the opposition, and what concerned us in the towns was that some of the country cousins did not seem to understand how much this was hurting us.

I drafted a letter to the local paper which admitted that this was a daft thing to do, but which turned the debate onto our charitable trust campaign issue.

The Executive asked me not to send it, but I did anyway, and am glad I did as it was a fighting defence and brought out all the vitriol and abuse of the opposition in published letters the following week.

Voters do not like Politicians insulting each other

The other thing I had been asking the Conservatives to do for many years was not to be rude about our opponents; on the doorsteps, people are fed up with politicians being rude about each other. When one of the most outspoken and aggressive Hertford old guard Tories said to me: *'Jim, we really must make sure we do not say rude things about the opposition because people do not like it'*, I realised that the party had at last begun to listen and change.

So we made a point on the doorstep of complimenting our opponents who were sitting councillors, and commending them for their hard work for the people of Hertford.

Having provoked our opponents to insult us in the press, I sent a final letter to the local paper which got top billing in the last issue before the election: it is time, I wrote, to stop the nonsense of pretending that all the candidates in the other parties are crooks, and that councils controlled by other parties never do anything good. I stated that all the Labour and Liberal Democrat candidates were good people who wanted the good of the Town and its people, as were our Conservative candidates.

I praised some of the things the Labour Town Council had done, and pointed out that we had also praised them in our manifesto material delivered to every household. I said we should compete on the best new ideas (and cited our Assured Shorthold Tenancy Key-Worker housing scheme for teachers) and we should stop the mud-slinging.

People stopped me in the street on this one, which apparently touched a cord in a lot of people.

Playing it for Laughs

So Peter Ruffles and I tried hard to change the tone of the election and set an example. We also played some of it for laughs, to see whether this would make any difference.

In one Ward that we had no hope of winning, Nik our candidate was a talented professional artist, and for our drop 48 hours before the election he did a cartoon of an old lady on a skateboard delivering Meals on Wheels (I had wanted her to be skating to the Citizens Advice Bureau, but this was felt to be a bit too close to the bone).

In Sele, the other ward we had no hope of winning, and where Helle my secretary was one of the candidates, we took a photo of her seven year old son with his football and put the caption *"Matt says please vote for my Mum, so Dad and me can watch the football when she is out at Council meetings".*

We had a market stall on Saturday for three weeks, featuring the planning application for the skatepark and the plans for the teachers housing; the MP joined us one week, and this was a good way of being seen and meeting people.

The team worked well together, even though we did not expect to get very far, and I think by and large we did all enjoy the campaign. In my diary the night before the 2003 election, I wrote that I expected to gain one more District seat to get us to 3 out of ten, and I hoped we might get to six Town seats out of sixteen.

Now we had to make sure our election administration was as good as it could be.

12
Election Administration

If you are standing for a party, you will probably not have to worry about the actual administration of the election. If you wonder how it all happens, or if you have to do it on your own, here is a potted guide:

Election Agent

You do not need an Agent, but if the party has one, then you probably have little to worry about. If you are your own Agent, then you have to take responsibility for the Election.

The key things to worry about are:

- deadlines
- election expenses
- making sure the literature has the proper imprint
- candidate behaviour
- donations

The Electoral Commission has an excellent website, and you can download the '**Guidance for Candidates and Agents**' document that tells you all you need to know in about 120 pages.

www.electoralcommission.org.uk

I flag the five issues above, because they are the ones that you need to watch. The completion of the Nomination Form, eligibility for election, forms to be completed and so on are straightforward, but you still need to keep your copy of the Guidance on your bedside table.

The dates and timings are crucial, and on one day when nominations closed, one of our signatories was found to be ineligible, and I had an hour to drive from Bishops Stortford to Hertford, get a valid signature, and get back to Bishops Stortford. We made it with two minutes to spare.

Election Expenses

We are very fortunate in this country that you cannot buy an election. There are very strict limits on what you can spend and the penalties for offences against the Representation of the People Act 1983 include fines of up to £5,000 and two years in prison.

The only problem is that you are not allowed enough money to pay for the printing and delivery of two leaflets, so you have to use volunteers to deliver, or do it yourself.

You need two leaflets, because you have to get an early leaflet out before the Postal Voting forms are sent out, and you need one close to the election because the voters will have forgotten you if you rely on the early leaflet.

You therefore have to watch the pennies, and if you have paid staff helping you, they must keep timesheets. The Guidance tells you what to do about rosettes left over from the last election, and the use of office space.

Certain things do not count as election spending, and these are:

- Facilities like school halls you can use as of right (but not the cost of preparing the hall)

- Your own time as a candidate, providing this is voluntary, in your own time, and free of charge, although I am not certain how it could be otherwise

- The publication (other than an advert) in a newspaper or magazine, a broadcast by the BBC or other licensed radio or TV operator

- Use of your home

- Use of a friend's home, provided you do not pay for it

- Using your own car or bicycle

- Using someone else's car or bicycle providing you do not pay for it

- Using your own computer

- Using your friend's computer, providing it was bought for personal use and you are not charged for using it

This is not a very long list, so watch out.

The Imprimatur

The Electoral Commission calls these 'Imprints'. All election publicity must carry an imprint, and if it does not, then the candidate's election can be challenged under S110(12) of the RPA 1983.

You need to be clear who the Promoter is, who is the Printer, and who the material is 'on behalf of'. The Commission gives a number of examples in the Guide, so for example for a party candidate you might have:

Printed by The Duplication Company **of** 107 Railway Street, Hertford SG14 1QQ. **Promoted by** Gordon Brown **of** 93 High Street, Hertford SG14 2QQ **on behalf of** the Raving Monster Loony Party **of** 183A West Street, Hertford SG14 3QQ.

For an Independent candidate using their own photocopier, the imprint might be:

Printed and promoted by Gordon Brown **of** 93 High Street, Hertford SG14 2QQ.

Every leaflet and poster must have this, and you might want to read the Guidance on websites and blogs.

Candidate Behaviour

It is obvious that a candidate should not try and bribe a voter, but you must also not 'treat' a voter with free food, drink or entertainment.

You must also be careful of what you do around Polling Stations. A group of your supporters outside a station could be seen as a form of undue influence by trying to intimidate. There is an Appendix to the Guidance which sets out guidelines for tellers at Poling Stations.

On Election Day you need to be careful with cars plastered in posters, and watch where they go.

Donations

You need to declare any donations in excess of £50, so it is important that you keep proper records of any donations and who makes them.

The election agent is legally responsible for the financial conduct of the candidate's campaign, but if you are your own Agent, then you need to read the Guidance.

You can only accept a donation from a 'permissible donor', and these are:

- An individual registered on a UK electoral register
- A Great Britain-registered political party
- A UK-registered company
- A UK-registered trade union
- A UK-registered building society
- A UK-registered friendly society
- A UK-registered limited liability partnership
- A UK-based unincorporated association

Your fans can make a donation to your Party, if you have one, but if this is passed on to you, it simply becomes a donation from the Party.

The Guidance gives examples of the forms you will have to complete, and the dates by which they must be submitted.

Not only can you appoint an Election Agent, but you can also Appoint Polling Agents and Counting Agents.

The Guidance tells you all about the procedures and what happens at the count, but there is nothing quite like the buzz of a whole load of political players and groupies waiting for the result of the match.

13
The Count

The ballot boxes are piled in the middle of the hall. The boxes are large plastic containers, and look a bit like kerbside recycling crates. Each box is opened and verified. You can watch this, and so can your Polling and Counting Agents. There are tables around the room where the votes are counted and bundled up, and you can watch the piles grow and try and guess the result.

The Polling Stations close at 10pm, and you can attend the sealing of the ballot boxes and thank the staff, but you can only do this at one Polling Station for obvious reasons. The boxes are then taken to the count.

In 2003 I went up to the count as usual, and watched the first boxes being emptied. I watched my Castle Ward boxes, and my impression was that I was getting about 30-40% of the vote. People asked me how we were doing, and I said quite sincerely I did not expect to be re-elected.

I stopped watching the boxes as it was too depressing. We all felt we had done the best we could, we had been honest as far as we could, we had tried to be decent and honourable and give credit where it was due, and we had tried to set an example by respecting our opponents: if politicians cannot respect each other, how can we expect the public to respect politicians?

By midnight we felt we had run a fair campaign, we had done all we could with the resources we had, and we were satisfied that whatever the result we had no grounds on which to reproach ourselves.

Recounts

At about 1.00am I was summoned to a recount in Kingsmead, the ward where Rob next door and Nik the artist were standing. The figures were amazing: Rob was well in and Nik was just above the popular and well respected Liberal Democrat who had represented the ward for many years. Nik was 14 votes ahead, and after two recounts the Liberal Democrats conceded victory.

We had captured two seats which had been Liberal Democrat for years: it was an outstanding victory and the MP and the Leader of the Council asked where the victorious candidates were for press photographs. I told them they were in bed because they did not expect to be elected; I was told to phone them and get them up to the count. I refused – I said I had promised these people there was no chance of them being elected, and I was now in serious trouble with them and their wives. This was not received well.

The next count was my own, and I was amazed to find that not only was I top of the poll, but my two Conservative colleagues had also been elected: the leader of the Labour party was heavily defeated, and we had captured two seats from Labour. We now had five of the ten Hertford seats. This just shows that you should be wary of jumping to conclusions when watching the verification.

At this point I took my wife Viv home, and when I came back I was told that not only had we captured all the seats in Bengeo Ward (we were now eight out of ten) but there was a recount in Sele ward where Helle, my hard-working secretary was standing. I went to monitor the recount and found that one of our two candidates was well in (now 9 out of 10) and Helle was six votes ahead of the sitting Labour councillors.

After the first recount this was reduced to five votes, but after the second recount it went back to six and the Labour party accepted defeat. We had ten out of ten and I now had to tell Helle she was a councillor: this result was totally unprecedented.

The whole team were excited, and it looked as though we would therefore capture the Town Council as well: the Town count was on Friday morning, so we all went to bed.

The Count for the Town Council

I had meetings in London on the Friday morning, so could not attend the count. The candidates kept me informed on the results as they were announced, and the first result was Castle (four out of four), then Bengeo (four out of four – including the 21 year old last minute pub barman candidate), then for Sele we captured two out of four – sadly our third candidate did not quite make it: the voters do like people who live in the ward, and Sue lived just outside.

We now had ten out of sixteen, a clear majority, and we had to start worrying about who we would appoint as mayor. There was no result yet on Kingsmead, where I was standing for the Town Council.

I had appointed 'Generals' for each area to run the campaign, organise the deliveries, the canvassing, and the final drop. I ran the Kingsmead campaign, as I wanted to let my colleagues do the door knocking in Castle where I was a sitting councillor; I reasoned that I would have the advantage of being known from the past four years, so they should have the opportunity to get themselves as well known as possible.

So I did nothing in Castle, and still came top of the poll. I worked hard in Kingsmead, I brought the MP, the MEP and the Leader of the Council to door knock with me, and I had been over the moon when all this work paid off and Rob and Nik were elected for the District Council (even though they did not really want to be).

As I was driving back to Hertford I had the call from the worried Castle Ward chairman: she had drawn the short straw to tell me the result in Kingsmead. The good news was that we had won three of the four seats, so now had thirteen out of sixteen seats on the town council. The bad news was that I was the one Conservative that had not been elected.

The team were all gobsmacked, as I had expected to be leader or Mayor on the Town Council to leave Peter free for his County Council work. I am afraid I simply laughed, as it was such a bizarre outcome. However, it left me free to work on the four projects, and to do what I could to help make the Leader-and-Cabinet option work better on East Herts Council.

Political life has a habit of being unpredictable.

With 42 seats out of 50, the Labour party was wiped out, and only seven Liberal Democrats and one Independent remained.

This was not good news for democracy. I wrote in my diary: *"I have started working on the Leader to adjust the organisation to cope with this unhealthy majority. Fortunately he is a good man and recognises the dangers and is keen to listen to new ideas."* I still think he is a good man, even though later I had to lead the attack to have him resign as Leader.

But for now I had to try and help some unexpectedly elected Councillors try and find their feet.

14
The Newly Elected Councillor

Matt, our young skateboard committee chairman, found himself an elected Councillor both of the Hertford Town Council, and East Herts Council. Neither he nor I expected he would be elected, and he had a high pressure job selling plywood.

Trying to fit everything in, he arrived a bit late for a Council Meeting in his work clothes, basically shorts, sandals and a tee-shirt.

This was not appreciated by the old guard, who believed that there are Standards that Must be Maintained, and Matt was unnecessarily embarrassed by the way it was handled. So for the next Town Council meeting he went in his DJ, which was even less appreciated.

Each Council and Party will have its own standards and way of doing things, and the Council Officers (the civil servants) will do all they can to help you.

Here are some of the things I noted:

- There are a lot of papers to read, and these will either come to you electronically, or be posted on a website with password access, or delivered to you in hard copy.

- It is better to try and chose the areas you want to work on, and let other people do the rest, otherwise you drown.

- You will do most of your discussion in Committees, so you do not have to worry if you have a fear of standing up and making a speech. In fact long speeches are discouraged, and although the public are generally allowed to attend Council Committee meetings, the atmosphere is fairly informal, and if you are used to discussions at a PTA, sports club, Guides or Operatic Society committee you will not find it very different.

- The full Council meetings are a farce, because all the important decisions are made behind closed doors, and full Council is a political meeting when you say rude things about your opponents and rubber stamp what has already been decided.

- The main meeting where important decisions will be made will be the Executive meetings, and you need to keep a close watch on these. There are tight timetables and short notice periods, and this is where important decisions are slipped past Councillors in the hope that they will not notice until it is too late. Watch these closely.

- You need to find an experienced old Councillor you can relate to who will give you help and advice. Your postbag will get you excited at first, but the older and wiser will help you differentiate between those who need help and those who are trying to use you as a pawn in a battle.

- Local Authority finance is not the same as private sector finance or accounting, but it is not that different, so do not let the Officers try and pull the wool over your eyes. The main difference is on what I would call 'depreciation', so it is worth getting your mind around how Local Authorities treat capital expenditure.

- I was amazed to discover in 1999 that I would get an annual allowance of £750 for postage and phonecalls. The total cost to the Council of the Members and their expenses was then about £75,000 per annum. That all changed with the Local Government Act 2000 and I found myself getting £10,000 a year as a Committee chair. You need to decide what you are going to do with the cash and who you are going to tell about it.

- The truest maxim is not 'a week is a long time in politics', but Lord Acton's old one: 'power tends to corrupt and absolute power tends to corrupt absolutely.' Make sure you have a trusted friend who will keep you humble when you start to think you have become a bit important by getting elected.

15
How Much Time does it Take?

How much time have you got?

The bare minimum is to attend full Council, which is probably five or six times a year, but may be monthly. If you fail to attend for a certain period, usually six months, you can be thrown off the Council.

The responsibilities then fall into four categories.

First, there will be the **decision making Meetings**, such as the Executive, which may be every six weeks. Then there will be Committees, such as the Planning Committee, or the Scrutiny Committees where you will discuss papers produced by Officers, make recommendations, and have an opportunity to influence the outcomes. Depending on how many Committees you are on, you may find yourself going to two, four or more meetings a month. Most important of all are the Party Group meetings. If you are not on the Planning Committee, it is probably going to be on average one a week if you want to have an impact.

Secondly, there will be **Community Meetings** that relate to your Ward. You may decide to have a Surgery where you make yourself available to your electors, which could be every month or every quarter, and may be on a Saturday morning. You may have some Community Forum that will cover a number of Wards, where members of the public can come and be informed and express opinions. Again, these might be six or eight times a year.

Thirdly, you may want to attend meetings or annual **meetings of significant Community Groups**, such as Residents' or Tenants' Associations, Sports Clubs, Charities, Faith Communities or Schools and Colleges.

Lastly, you will get a range of **unsolicited invitations** from organisations, companies, property developers, community pressure groups and single issue campaigns, who all have a particular agenda they want you to support.

This therefore brings us back to the first question: *how much time have you got to give to this?*

On a **Parish or Town Council** it is clear that the work has to be done in the evenings, so that Councillors with full-time jobs can participate fully in the work of the Council.

On a **County Council** it would be impossible to do the work in the evenings, so you need to expect to put aside two days a week or so to be a County Councillor.

On a **District Council** with Planning Responsibilities, like East Herts Council, it is not so clear cut. My own view was that if the Cabinet and Officers got their act together, the work could all be done in the evenings. The range of activities is very wide, but with better organisation and focus it could be very much more efficient.

At our younger son's graduation I sat next to the Leader of a District Council with a similar profile to East Herts in the North of England. He told me he was a partner in a firm of solicitors, and as Leader he went in to the Council for one afternoon a week. They had a higher ranking from the Audit Commission than East Herts had at the time.

Hertford local politics was dominated in the mid-nineties by John Sartin. John in my view represented the best in local politics, and he dominated East Herts Council, running it efficiently as Leader from the upper floor of his toyshop in town, and making few enemies in the process.

Nothing much has changed in the Council workload since John Sartin's time, apart from the sale of the Council Housing, which has actually reduced the scale of operations. As a result of the 2000 Local Government Act East Herts now pays Members and Cabinet Members £500,000 per annum and you cannot help feeling that the Leader and Cabinet probably feel obliged to create work for the Executive, simply to justify the amount they are now paying themselves.

If you want to see the Council at work, you will need to visit the Council Offices during working hours, and this will mean talking to the Officers (the staff) who do the work.

16
Officers and Members

Just as it was in *Yes, Minister*, the relationship between the Sir Humphreys and the Jim Hackers is still the biggest problem in government. My take on this is that in the private sector we ask: "*How can we get this done?*" whereas in the public sector they ask: "*Are we allowed to get this done?*"   No officer will do anything unless they are sure it is permissible.

The Local Government Act 2000 brought in Cabinet government to most local authorities. In fact it gave you four options, none of which was to retain the committee structure that had worked well enough for 150 years. Most Councils chose the 'Leader-and-Cabinet' option, where the Leader selects six or seven Councillors to be 'Portfolio Holders' and look after specific areas of Council Work as members of the 'Executive', or Cabinet.

It is one thing to try and get things done with 646 MPs, but what works in the Commons looks a bit daft with 50 councillors. It has generally led to the marginalisation of the back benchers, as we found later when our Back Bench Committee started doing some research by phoning our counterparts in other local Councils around the country.

Our Leader relished the opportunity to sort out the Sir Humphrey of East Herts, so as soon as the new structure was implemented, he sacked him.

What happened next is still not entirely clear to an ordinary councillor like me, but officers and cabinet members reach for expensive solicitors in a way that makes my eyes water, and would quickly bankrupt me if I did it at work.

What we do know is that the final bill was well over £1m, as the other top Directors were told to re-apply for their jobs, allegedly on the basis of legal advice given to our Leader.

When the dust settled, we had three Directors none of whom was in charge of the whole show. When I asked the Leader about this, he said he wanted to 'let the best man win'. Since two of them were women, and since the two women quickly saw off the one man, and then fell out with each other, I am not sure what he meant.

I wish I had been more forceful in telling him we would never do such a daft thing in the private sector, but I was new, and I thought the public sector might be different in some way. It is not.

Manager or Politician?

Actually I think the real problem was that the Leader wanted to run the officers <u>and</u> the politicians. I did challenge him on this one, and consistently told him he could be an officer <u>or</u> a politician, but not both. If he was enjoying being de facto chief executive of the Council and its officers, then who was doing the politics and minding the elected Members' shop?

With the greatest respect to my elected colleagues, many of them had never run companies or organisations of any size, and they were elected to make political decisions, not executive decisions. The calibre of elected Member in the lower rungs of local government is generally not very high, as you can guess from the difficulty all parties have in getting decent candidates to stand for election.

I think the best model for a newly elected Member is to think of the role of a **non-Executive Company Director**. The non-exec has no job to do within the organisation, and therefore has to rely on instincts and experience. You will need to find time to call in at the Council Offices and talk to the staff. Try and guess what they are not telling you, and get a feel for what is going on that you can balance against the written papers you are given.

I was accused of always thinking the worst about a situation, but in business there is no other way, and sadly the Council was no different. Suspicion about how a tender was awarded, for example, led me to discover that there was no tender opening procedure and left officers open to accusations of being in a position to pass on bid prices to competing bidders.

If the Leader and Cabinet try and discourage you from talking to Officers, then you can be pretty sure that something is going on. Talk to every officer you can, and make every effort to sniff out what they are up to.

Employed Officers do the work, Elected Members do the politics, and there needs to be a very clear division of responsibility and understanding of what each other does and who manages what.

If you do come against a problem, then if you are an elected party Member, the forum to discuss this in is the Party *Group Meeting* behind closed doors.

17
Working as a Group

I discovered that our Conservative Party Group had no constitution, so we were not sure how we should go about making improvements to the way we worked together, and, nobody knew how to get rid of the Leader.

The **Party Group Meeting** of the elected Members is the most important meeting of all for any Councillor of any Party, as this is where you can try and get things done, or make your reputation, depending on your motivations or ambitions.

Your Group will generally meet before full Council to plot how to ambush the other side, avoid embarrassing questions or accusations, give a good story to the media, and generally make sure the Party is on target to win the next election. The mechanics of whipping (insistence on voting the Party line) will vary from Council to Council.

There will be regular other Group meetings which look at policy issues and make decisions. Some Leaders look at these meetings as being a time to make sure all the Councillors are kept fully informed, but do as the Cabinet has already decided. Others will be more democratic and welcome the input and experience of all the Councillors.

The only problem with welcoming input at Group Meetings is that many Councillors love the sound of their own voices and these meetings can go on for hours unless there is tight and focussed chairing.

You will have maximum impact in the Group if:

(a) you are brief

(b) you make a good point nobody else has made

(c) you wait until about two-thirds through the debate before making your first point.

The main Group Dynamic in the ruling Party Group is probably naked ambition, and while it is probably necessary to pay Councillors allowances, I noticed that with the 2000 Local Government Act, money also became an issue. At one election for a Chair of Committee, the current Chair was alleged to have been asking Members for their vote, as the candidate needed the additional allowance as Chair to maintain a basic standard of living after retirement.

In opposition, the dynamic is probably different, but reports that leak out from other party Group Meetings indicate that this is still where the real action takes place.

Decisions behind Closed Doors

The main problem with making decisions behind closed doors is that your constituents cannot see how hard you fought on an issue. Everybody knows that when choices have to be made, it is impossible to please everybody. This is much less of a problem if people can _see_ that their point of view has been championed in the forum that has to make the decision.

Having some sort of token debate in full Council is not the same when you know that the real battle has taken place behind closed doors, and the losers have to troop in like lemmings and vote for the agreed party line.

There will be issues of principle when normally your Group will probably allow you to vote against the Party, but you need to get permission first. The opposition may ask for a 'Recorded Vote' when you have to shout out 'For' or 'Against' or 'Abstain' and your vote then becomes a matter of public record.

Holding the Reins of Power

The Group Meeting of the ruling party is where the real power lies. So our new Leader tried to ensure that it would be impossible to remove him within his first four years. Well, we think that was the situation, but without a Constitution nobody was quite sure.

To the obvious irritation of some of the older Members, I insisted we must have a Constitution. We discovered later that there is in fact a standard Constitution for Conservative Groups, and after the upsets I understood from the Conservative Party hierarchy that they had no idea how far the Leader had gone to try and make himself impregnable.

I have some sympathy with the Leader. If you give up opportunities to earn more money, you ought to have some security of tenure. However, I am simply not convinced that a politician ought to be doing management work. If you want to do that, then be an elected Mayor.

So make sure you have it all written down, and make sure that you do not need to have an impossible hurdle to get over in making major decisions that are likely to be resisted by the Leader and Cabinet.

Since any important decisions are made behind closed doors, the media have to sniff around and try and find a chatty Councillor who will spill the beans about what actually happened in the Group Meeting.

18
The Media

One of my worst ideas was to try and employ some PR support for the Conservative Group on East Herts Council. At the time, the editor of the local paper was not a fan of the Conservatives, and it was difficult to get any positive press coverage.

I talked to a local PR company, and asked them if they could help. The Party Group reluctantly agreed to go along with the idea, but when we submitted the first press release, the front page story was not our story, but the fact that the Conservatives had resorted to employing a spin doctor.

If you think you can fight an election campaign through the local newspaper, then think again.

I twice wrote a letter of complaint to Lord Iliffe, the press baron who owns the local paper and takes the Conservative whip in the House of Lords. After the second time, the Chief Executive of the Newspaper Group pleaded with me to speak to him first before I complained to his boss next time.

The next time occurred when the paper wrote a large back page feature about an alleged bust-up I was supposed to have had with another local Councillor. I was chair of the Community Forum, and one of the Hertford Councillors had a medical problem and it appeared he may have forgotten to take his medication.

I had to take him outside before the meeting because of the aggressive way he was talking to the Council Officers. Outside, I told him if he came back inside, I would call the police and get him thrown out.

After a sensible discussion, he promised to behave. On the understanding that if he said one word during the meeting I would call the police, we went back into the meeting together. When we walked in, he made some loud comment, but other than that, he kept his promise, and the meeting was uneventful.

A Right to Silence?

Just before the paper went to press, I had a call from a reporter. I was asked what had happened before the meeting. I refused to say anything. As far as I was concerned, this Councillor had a private problem which he was dealing with, and it was not for me to comment, nor for the paper to publicise.

The article basically made a number of assumptions which were demonstrably untrue, and the tone of the article was in my view completely inappropriate given the truth of what had happened.

This time I emailed the Chief Executive and said that not only would I complain to his boss, but I would also be making a formal complaint to the Press Complaints Commission.

The paper back-tracked, and I was allowed to draft the apology to be printed on the back page. I was also invited to lunch to meet the editor and the senior staff of the paper.

It was the discussion at this lunch that I found so concerning. The attitude of the editor was that I should disclose all the facts to the newspaper, and they should decide what should be printed. It was my duty, they believed, to disclose the Councillor's personal problems to the press, and for them to decide what is in the public interest.

There is this curious conflict within journalism. Papers can only exist if they can sell advertising, yet many journalists want to have the highest ethical standards. These two are difficult bedfellows. Sup with journalists with a very long spoon.

The following is advice I have been given, and I commend it to you:

- nothing you say to a journalist is <u>ever</u> 'off the record'

- journalists have a job to do, and they are not your friend who will do you a favour

- never say "No Comment"

- don't make jokes, and don't lie

- If you don't know the answer, say so, but promise to get back to them quickly with an answer, and make sure you do

- Say what you want to say as briefly as possible, and then stop, and refuse to be bullied by silences

There is no way that I want to argue for one minute that the press should be muzzled, and the future of many parts of the world will depend on the freedom of the press.

But whose job is it to blow the whistle on corruption and bad judgement and incompetence? Opposition politicians are there to watch over what is going on, but the current system also expects members of the ruling party to monitor what their colleagues are up to. The process is called *'Scrutiny'*, and it is the way in which elected Councillors are supposed to hold the Executive to account.

19
Scrutiny

I am a governor of Richard Hale School in Hertford, which was formally the old Hertford Grammar School and counts the Bishop of London among its alumni. I am also a governor of Haileybury College, which is near Hertford, and is one of the top Public Schools in the country.

The two schools have radically different problems when it comes to recruiting staff, and when discussing this with a former Head Teacher of Richard Hale, he said he believed that it was the high cost of housing in Hertford that caused difficulties in recruitment in the public sector. Haileybury, as a Boarding School, had its own housing for teachers.

I wondered if I could use my property knowledge to help find a solution that could become a good election issue. It was one of the Council Officers who suggested a solution using a form of key worker housing and Assured Shorthold Tenancies that had been pioneered by an NHS Trust in London.

At the time we had a potential site at Mill Road in Hertford, and I was able to persuade the Leader that we should use the social housing element on the site for such a scheme, giving first priority to teachers.

We therefore went to the polls in Hertford with one of our four key manifesto pledges being cheap housing for teachers.

I do not understand to this day why the Leader and Executive then tried to exclude me from any discussion or involvement with the Mill Road project. I was promised a site of the plans and draft agreements, but nothing was given to me until it was pretty much too late.

Suddenly we were told it was all stitched up, and there was no commitment to teachers. I had no alternative but to *'call-in'* the decision.

'Call-in' is a process where the Executive has to justify to Councillors a decision that has been made. I used call-in twice, and cannot recall any other Conservative using the process. Although this is what the Act expects you to do, many of the Party felt I was being a traitor.

Scrutiny is very difficult where there is a large majority. In East Herts in 2003-7 it was 42 seats out of 50, and without any effective opposition, who holds the Executive to account?

On Mill Road, we had a hearing and a member of the Executive had to try and justify the decision not to give teachers a priority when the ten Hertford Members had been elected to do precisely that. Fortunately the Executive backed down, but they did not like being challenged.

Hung Councils

Power tends to corrupt ...... and there is no question that large majorities do not lead to good government. Scrutiny can only work if you stand a reasonable chance of persuading some people to stand up to the Party machine. Minority administrations and hung councils probably deliver better government.

The Conservatives in East Herts complained bitterly about the four years when they had a minority but were still the largest party. Why? *Because they had to work hard to persuade*

*Councillors **in public** of the merits of a particular case.* They could not use patronage and closed doors to make their life easy.

Whether it is Parliament or Council Chamber, how you hold the Executive to account is the major problem. Scrutiny will only work if you have a reasonable chance of out-voting the Executive.

If you believe that public debate is the right way to make good decisions, then one way to ensure this is to have a good number of 'floating voters', or Independent Councillors who hold the balance of power.

Scrutiny is supposed to be where the Back Benchers make their contribution to the democratic process. However, what has killed the enthusiasm of many Back Benchers has been the fact that they are expected to do what they are told and not rock the boat if they want to get ahead.

Being a Party Back Bencher, which most newly elected Councillors will be, can be a frustrating experience.

20
Backbenchers have No Fun

It will depend on the make-up of the Council, but when you are first elected you are most likely to be a Back Bencher even if you are a member of the majority party.

Backbenchers are elected Councillors who have no other task than to represent the electors in their Ward. The Councillors with the jobs will try and convince you that this is a noble calling and the bedrock on which local democracy is built.

This may be true up to a point, but the voters expect you to do things and make things happen, but as a Backbencher you learn very quickly that there are limits to what you can do.

When the Backbenchers start getting restless, the best advice is to give them something to do. Our Backbench Committee tried to get the Cabinet Members to have a small group of Backbenchers that they would work with in decision making on their Portfolio. Some Cabinet Members tried to do this, but others ignored it.

You quickly realise that the only Councillors who have any real fun are the Leader and Cabinet Members.

Perhaps 'fun' is the wrong word. Perhaps what I really mean is that Backbenchers generally have no power, unless the Council is a hung Council or the Parties are fairly evenly matched.

As a newly elected Councillor you therefore have to look at the situation in which you find yourself and work out how you are going to avoid frustration or disillusionment.

If you are in the **ruling Party**, you have to decide how far you are going to put your personal ambition above the needs of your Ward.

If you are in an **opposition Party**, you need to work out how far you are going to put party politics and the desire to win the next election above the needs of your Ward.

It was wrestling with these issues that eventually led me towards seeing the advantages of being an Independent, where my sole concern can be the needs of my Ward, and making sure that we have open debates about contentious issues.

You may see things differently, but one of the hardest things about being a Party Backbencher is the inability to be open about the way in which decisions are reached. People complain that 'the Council' or 'their Councillor' never listens to them. *We always listen*, but we do not always agree with what is being said.

Generally the complaint that people do not listen is under-pinned by the assumption that if you listen to what I say, you will agree with my argument. The frustration for the Backbench Councillor is that often you do agree with what is being said, but the Group decided otherwise, and your complainant cannot know how hard you actually pushed their argument in the debate.

If the frustration of being a powerless Backbencher is more than you can take, you can always leave the Party and start your own.

21
Starting your own Party

The idea of resigning when you make a mistake or something goes wrong appears to have gone out of fashion. Although we won the battle to get the Leader to go, we lost the war when the Deputy Leader was elected Leader and business went on as usual.

As a prime mover in the attempts to find a way out of the mess, I felt my failure to get a real change and an apology to the voters meant I had to take the consequences. I could not in good conscience defend the record of the Conservative Administration, and I felt I had failed the voters.

I am not quite sure how the idea came about, as I did not ever think the couple of Independent Members in 2003-7 on East Herts Council were particularly effective. Things are different now, with the two new Independents forming the only fighting opposition that I can see, although it is a real struggle against so many.

Somehow I was introduced to the idea that standing as an Independent might be a better way of being a Councillor, with the freedom to bring issues into the open.

I talked to a number of local politicians that I respected, who were not in the Conservative party. I researched a bit, and decided that one way forward would be to start my own political party. One of the Cabinet Members from Bishop's Stortford kindly took the trouble to send me a detailed account of the old

Ratepayers Association, in an effort to dissuade me from going down that route.

A number of interested people met in the White Horse pub in Castle Street one evening, and out of this came the name 'East Herts People'.

The Electoral Commission

In order to register with the Electoral Commission, you need to have a Constitution and some Officers. All of this is clearly set out on the website www.electoralcommision.com and if you want a Constitution as a starting point, then go to the East Herts People website www.ehpeople.org and download ours and hack it around for your own use.

The Commission require regular returns, and are good at reminding you. They are very strict, and when I failed to send in one set of accounts on time, they fined me £500 and would not listen to any pleading about the poverty and lack of resources of small political parties.

A Political Party or an Independent?

People cannot understand why East Herts People is a registered Political Party, but not a political party. I try and explain that it is an enabling organisation, whose sole purpose is to get *Independents* elected. There are advantages in being registered. However, EHP is not a political party that wants to see the East Herts People Party providing the Leader and Cabinet of East Herts Council, nor does it have specific policies other than to promote the best for each Ward.

When we put up 13 candidates for East Herts Council in 2007, against my better judgment I agreed we should stand as East Herts People and not as Independents. One of my former Council colleagues, Deborah Clark, who had been a Cabinet Member on East Herts Council, decided to stand as an

Independent, and not as East Herts People, and so did her husband Nigel. I think they made the better choice.

They were both elected, but none of the East Herts People candidates got in. They both worked very hard for their victories, and they were outstanding candidates, so I do not think their success and our failure is in itself an argument in favour of standing as an Independent rather than as a local issue political party candidate. It will all depend on the candidates and the circumstances.

There are a number of good examples of local issue political parties, like Better Bedford, and this may well be the best way to achieve your aims. But a local issue political party is still a political party, and you will still have the problems of working as a group.

Only an Independent avoids this conflict of interest, but probably only by working together can you achieve anything significant. However, co-operation between Independents does not necessarily mean you have to give up independence.

Problems to Overcome

We had a good time in the 2007 election, and East Herts People had a great team of candidates: John Barber, Anna Fenton, John Brady, Tom Busby, Mike Edwards, Stephen Froud, Viv and me in Hertford, David Perman in Ware, Debbie leMay in Buntingford, Paul Lacey in Stanstead Abbotts, Alison Juniper in Hertford Rural North and Mary Wilkinson in Much Hadham.

David and Debbie stood for their Town Councils, and Debbie was successful. Viv did better than I did, and if it had not been for a friend of ours who stood in the ward for the Labour Party, she might have been elected.

We spent up to the limit, and when we found we had no funds left to buy poles for posters, we came up with the idea of getting people to put out their wheelie-bins on the pavement with posters attached. This led to the threat of an injunction from East Herts Council, so we knew that at least somebody was following our blog and website. I therefore rented six wheelie-bins, pasted on slogans and posters, put them on top of cars, and drove them around town.

While it was a disappointing result, it enabled us to see a number of problems that we have to overcome if we are to make any headway and get significant numbers elected in 2011.

The biggest problem is the **lack of volunteers**. The main parties have their Party Members who will do leaflet deliveries, canvassing, market stalls and so on during the election. Without this infrastructure, you have a real disadvantage. You are not allowed to spend much during an election, so you cannot pay people to do this work for you.

Secondly, you do not have **access to all the analysis** of the Ward or constituency that the major parties have built up over the years. When you have purchased a copy of the Electoral Roll, you need to analyse it to find how many leaflets you need to print, and where the largest number of voters are focussed.

I normally do this by inserting two columns in the spreadsheet you get from the Electoral Registration Office. One is for the number of voters and the other is for the number of housing units.

So if the first line is 2 High Street, and there are three voters in the house, you look down the column and count up the number of voters in High Street, and put this on the first line in the 'Number of Voters' column. You then look down and see that the last number in High Street is 27, so there are probably 27 houses in the street. Not every house has a voter, but you do not have time to tell your deliverers which houses or flats to miss. It is all or nothing.

On the first line you then have two numbers against '2 High Street'. You then delete all the lines below which have a 'High Street' address and move on to the next street, or block of flats and do the same process.

At the end, the total of the 'Number of Voters' column should be the same as the original total of voters. You now also have a total for the number of leaflets you have to print (as you only deliver one to each house or flat), and you can identify the streets with the largest numbers of voters.

All of this is time consuming, but needs to be done.

A third major problem is that people want to know **what Independents stand for**. Conservatives, Labour, Greens, Lib-Dems all have a brand that is recognisable, but Independents have no strap line or obvious unique selling point.

It is going to be a hard march back to the days when local election candidates were all people who were well-known in the community as *people*, and therefore voters knew what they were voting for because they were voting for a *person* not a party.

I realised that we had a lot to learn. I felt that there must be many people in a similar position to us, but I had no idea where to start.

Then I read a book by Barack Obama.

22
The Benefit of Researchers

I was on a plane back from a business trip to South Africa in the summer of 2008, and was reading Barack Obama's book *The Audacity of Hope.* I was surprised that he had started small with meetings of two or three people in a home, but most importantly he had found ways to use young people to harness the power of the internet to fight his election campaigns.

I worried that by the next election in 2011 voters would have forgotten the Independents who had stood in 2007. How could we keep the momentum going? I decided to stand as an Independent in the County Council election in 2009, but stand against an unbeatable sitting councillor to avoid getting elected.

I lived in the Hertford St Andrews Division comprising Castle and Sele Wards, and this would be an ideal seat to contest, as my old friend and colleague Peter Ruffles, the sitting Councillor, had such a large personal following that he could easily stand as an Independent and get elected with many more votes than I could ever get. With the Conservative vote as well, he was invincible.

Obama had an army of researchers to help him. I wondered if I could employ a part-time political researcher for my County Council campaign?

The researcher could also try and answer some of the questions I had about how we try and involve more young people in local politics, and how we could best push the arguments for a strong group of Independents as a better way of doing local government.

I had no idea what to pay a political researcher, but I put an advert in the local paper to see what response I would get. I was in South Africa again when the advert came out, and my office phoned me to say they were being inundated by applicants who had a load of questions my PA could not answer.

When I got back I found there were 85 applicants, and I sorted them into three piles. In the first pile – the pile with the most interesting applicants – were three young graduates in politics and economics or associated subjects. One was a Conservative and two were Lib Dems. I decided to start by interviewing these three.

What they had to tell me was fascinating, and I discovered that many researchers work as Interns for peanuts, simply to get experience. I worried that if they did come and work for me, they would never get a job again with their party of natural preference. They all assured me this would not be a problem.

They were each different, and since I could not decide, I offered them all a job, and they all accepted.

Laura worked full-time for me, and she was appointed as Team Leader. She had worked in David Cameron's office for a bit, and joined us in February 2009 after a temporary assignment in a Conservative MPs office in Cambridgeshire. Livia was doing part-time casework for an inner London Lib Dem MP, and James had just graduated, and they both worked part-time.

Part of the deal was that they must write a diary that we would publish, so that other people could get the benefit of this research project. These diaries, edited only slightly to remove a few actionable comments, are attached as Appendices to this book.

I will not steal their thunder about what happened in the election, and the two by-elections, and I will let them tell you in their own words what they found out from the public response, but I want to record my thanks to them for all their hard work, and for what I learned through their efforts.

Standing as an Independent is a tough job. You have little information to go on, you have to do your own research to find out about deliveries, you have little help or advice on the technicalities of the election process, your only helpers are friends and family, you are not allowed to spend much money, and the press and media are unreliable.

How do you do it?

23
Fighting as an Independent

My main conclusion from the 2009 County Council campaign was that as an Independent I simply did not have enough time to engage with the voters.

The limit on spending means that without an army of volunteers you have to do much of your own deliveries. I am very grateful to those who helped, but the current system is weighted in favour of the established parties.

Here are some simple reforms I would like to see:

- The Postal Voting forms should be sent out with a folded A4 leaflet from every candidate

- In every Polling Station there should be an A3 poster on the wall from each candidate setting out their election manifesto

People expect the candidates to knock on their door and talk to them. How many hours are there in an election period when this can be done? People will generally not open their doors after dark, many people are not back from work until at least 6pm and generally parties are reluctant to door knock on Sundays.

This leaves Saturdays (although interruptions during football matches are not appreciated) and no more than three hours a day, say 25 hours a week.

In five minutes I can generally get somebody to see the advantage of being Independent, but you do not have to be a great mathematician to calculate the impossibility of speaking to every voter in the time available.

The problem with market stalls or going round the pubs and shops is that you cannot distinguish who is in your Ward and who is not, which is why you are really stuck with knocking on the voters' doors.

*The main parties want people to vote for a brand, but if you believe that you should be voting for a **person** not a **party**, then the only way forward is for the distribution of manifestos to become a public responsibility.*

Wear your Rosette

If you are door knocking, then there has to be a way for the voter to know immediately that you are an election candidate. This means wearing a rosette, the time honoured badge of a candidate or political party supporter. Since there is no brand for Independents, we designed a rosette that was green, white and light blue, and had in the middle; "Vote Independent for a Change".

It would be good if the non-party candidates could agree on a brand image, but getting Independents to do something together is like herding cats. It is in the nature of Independents not to be organised, but some recognizable identity would be a help.

A National Problem

Another conclusion of the campaign is that without a strong campaign issue, the turnout rate is unlikely to rise very much. Some people think we should try compulsory voting as they do in Australia. However, abstention is just as much a vote, but the level of abstention in this country indicates a serious problem with the system.

Some Councils have experimented with opening Polling Stations on a number of days, but unless there is some attempt to give voters useful information about the candidates, and there is a strong campaign issue, I cannot see the apathy or abstention rate declining.

I think there is now agreement that the low turnout rates in local elections is a national problem that has to be addressed, so I am reasonably optimistic that there will be some gradual changes that will help Independents to get elected.

The Ward as a Community

The third main conclusion was something that the researchers had highlighted to me: the Ward, which elects Councillors, is an abstract idea and has no identity. For this reason there is no accountability for Councillors between elections, other than to their party.

I think there is some mileage here for the future, and the researchers experimented with producing an individual Ward Newsletter for each of the four Wards in Hertford.

We have almost completed the construction of a website and hope to launch a model in 2010 that could be used all over the country as a way of developing communications within a Ward. This could begin to build some form of real community to whom Councillors could be more accountable.

A much more fundamental problem is the problem of the financing of election campaigns.

24
Financing your Campaign

Within a few hours of the local paper printing the news of the formation of East Herts People in 2006, I had a phonecall from a local property developer offering to give substantial financial support to the party.

I realised this would be the kiss of death if news got out, so I refused to accept any money and decided that initially I had to finance the party myself. This is a matter of public record, as all donations over a certain size have to be declared.

I acted as Election Agent for the thirteen candidates in 2007, and was amazed when in 2009 one of those candidates told me the candidates thought the cost of the election was paid to the Election Agent by the local authority.

If you are going to stand as an Independent, you are going to have to pay for your campaign. In a Ward of 6,000 voters you can spend £600 plus 5p per voter, a total of £900. If you stand for Parliament you can spend £7,150 plus 5p or 7p per voter (depending on the type of constituency) during the short campaign period. So in a borough constituency of 55,000 voters you cannot spend more than £9,900.

You must be very careful that you do not overspend, but the concern must be that there are good candidates out there who are put off from standing because of the cost of a campaign, miniscule as it is compared to United States standards.

I wonder if a possible way forward for Independents is to get the support of community organisations for their candidacy? A donation of £100 from a local amenity group, or a neighbourhood watch, or a faith community is an enormous help, and could also lead to offers of help with deliveries. You can be completely open about such donations, and put up the details on your website or blog.

Spend as much as you can before the election period, so that the expenditure does not count in full. Find a friend of a friend who can do you a cheap website and help you get blogging if you have not yet found out how to do it.

The more people involved in helping you, the more quality support you will get, and quality support is the sort that gives verbal recommendation through the community networks.

25
The Independent Network

Livia kept on at me about going to this meeting at the end of September 2009. I had no idea what it was about, and it was at 2pm on a Friday afternoon when I had planned to be off early to go away for the weekend.

After the by-elections, and the researchers contracts were completed, Laura went off to work for another MP, but Livia had nothing immediately to go on to. I asked Livia to continue working one or two days a week through August and September 2009 to keep the East Herts People website and communications going.

She continued to keep an eye on the national scene for me, and was monitoring the website of the Independent Network which promotes the case for Independent Members of Parliament.

In the end, I found that I had a couple of hours to spare that Friday afternoon, so had no good reason to refuse Livia's enthusiastic promotion of this meeting in a PR company's office in North London.

We arrived a bit late, and I found myself in a jam packed room, with Martin Bell and Esther Rantzen in one corner, and an interesting mix of people from all over the country.

Livia and I had to sit in another corner at the front of the room, and there was a lively debate going on about how people could be encouraged and supported to stand for Parliament in these unprecedented times, when the stock of MPs and politicians generally was about as low as it could get.

There was debate about whether or not IN should register as a political party. What do Independents stand for? How do you fight an election as an Independent?

It was clear to Livia and me that although IN had supported about ten Independent candidates in 2005, we were a couple of years ahead in terms of grappling with some of the practical problems.

Inevitably I spoke out on a number of issues, and at the end of the meeting Brian Ahearne, the co-ordinator of IN asked for three people to form a National Executive to give support and encouragement, and take responsibility for making strategic decisions. This was about the only time there was dead silence in the room.

Then one person pointed and said: "That bloke in the corner with the glasses, I think he ought to be on the Executive. He seems to know what he is talking about." I looked behind me and realised that I must be the bloke in the corner he was pointing at. I could see no good reason not to share what we had been learning, so agreed.

Steve Ford, a doctor and PPC for Hexham in Northumberland, and his daughter Daisy, and Neville Watson from Tottenham, standing against David Lamy MP, and finally Livia were then also nominated to the National Executive.

The meeting believed that a first task for the Executive was to draft a Code of Conduct for Independent MPs. Martin Bell did a first draft, we have all had a go at them, and these are now the Bell Principles, which are included as Appendix I.

But can Independents really be effective in local government? Can they be effective in the House of Commons? Can they help create better communities and better politics?

26
Can Independents be Effective?

I was amazed to discover that there are over 2,000 Independent Councillors in England and Wales, about 7.5% of the total. In Scotland, Independents form the third largest grouping after SNP and Labour, with over 15% of the total.

There are 183 crossbench peers in the House of Lords, and three Independent Mayors in local authorities. Ken Livingstone was elected an Independent Mayor of London in 2000,

There were two directly elected Independent MPs in the 2005 General Election – Richard Taylor and Dai Davies. Trish Law is an Independent Member of the Welsh Assembly, and Margo MacDonald of the Scottish Parliament.

Scotland seems to be leading the way, as three Councils in Scotland have an Independent majority, and eleven Scottish Councils have an Independent coalition.

What seems to be agreed is that having Independents in the mix can make decisions harder, because the case has to be made, and Councillors have to *think*. If a small group can make decisions and then know the rest are obliged to support them, the quality of debate declines. The willingness of those with doubts to argue an opposite view will gradually evaporate.

We have no idea what changes an increase in the number of Independent Councillors and MPs will make. What we do know is that voters are unhappy with what we have at present, so anything that improves the quality of debate and the flow of information and the involvement of voters has to be an improvement.

An Independent is answerable only to the people in the Ward or Constituency, so there is no conflict of interest with a Party hierarchy.

On the other hand, an Independent cannot hope to be an expert on every issue, and there is an advantage in being part of a team that may include elected members with specialist knowledge.

However, if that expert knowledge is only made available to a small group of people who debate behind closed doors, then the separation between voter and elected member is increased.

We have to find a better way, and on the doorstep we are told:

- Voters want to know why and how decisions are made
- Voters want the opportunity to be listened to, and then want to know how their views have been taken into account
- Voters want politicians who are transparent and trustworthy, and willing to speak the truth, however unpopular it may be
- Voters are fed up with politicians who are rude to each other
- Voters want politicians who put the public interest above their own interests

I would want to argue that Independents have a better chance of meeting these aspirations than those who have a higher loyalty to a political party.

As a result of the work of Martin Bell and the Independent Network, we now have a set of Principles behind which Independent Councillors and MPs can unite.

Will this make for more effective government?

I believe it could begin to make a difference, and if you agree with me, *why not stand for election as an Independent yourself?*

Most books can be summarised in a couple of sentences, and this one is no different. My thesis is really this:

- You need political parties in a Chamber of 646, but not in a Town or Parish Council of 15 and probably not in a District Council of 50

- Political Parties do not like Hung or Minority-led Councils, as it means they have to work much harder to win arguments in public; but more open debate makes for better government, so the more Independents there are, forcing parties into a minority, the better

- With the declining calibre of party members and party politicians, one way to improve the calibre of politicians is to encourage good people to stand as Independents

- New technology can help in getting more openness, more public debate, more involvement of the electorate, and better election processes

The best resource available to help you as an Independent Councillor is undoubtedly the Independent Group Office at the Local Government Association, Smith Square, London SW1P 3HZ. Do have a look at their website, and check out their resources on www.independentgroup.lga.gov.uk

If there is anything I can do to help or encourage you, then do contact me at jim@ehpeople.org. If you have read this far, you obviously have a concern for your community! I wish you every success in your efforts to improve the way we do our politics.

Appendix 1
The Bell Principles

In a strategy meeting of the Independent Network ('IN') in September 2009, the former Independent MP Martin Bell suggested a set of principles for Independent elected representatives. IN members were so impressed by the principles they agreed to adopt them.

The Bell Principles were edited by the Executive for clarity. They are seen as a 'living document' and will be constantly reviewed and updated to ensure they're relevant for future generations.

The Bell Principles build upon Lord Nolan's Principles of 1995.

All IN endorsed candidates must abide by to the Bell Principles.

THE BELL PRINCIPLES

We will:

1. abide wholeheartedly by the spirit and letter of the Seven Principles of Public Life set out by Lord Nolan in 1995: *selflessness, integrity, objectivity, accountability, openness, honesty and leadership*

2. be guided by considered evidence, our real world experience and expertise, our constituencies and our consciences

3. be free from the control of any political party, pressure group or whip

4. be non-discriminatory, ethical and committed to pluralism

5. make decisions transparently and openly at every stage and level of the political process, enabling people to see how decisions are made and the evidence on which they are based

6. listen, consulting our communities constantly and innovatively

7. treat political opponents with courtesy and respect, challenging them when we believe they are wrong, and agreeing with them when we believe they are right

8. resist abuses of power and patronage and promote democracy at every level

9. work with other elected Independents as a Group with a chosen spokesperson

10. claim expenses, salaries and compensation openly so the public can judge the value for money of our activities

Appendix 2
Laura's Diary

Laura read History and Politics at the University of Exeter, and graduated in 2007. She has worked in politics both in Westminster and in a local constituency setting. From March to July 2009 she worked full-time for East Herts People and acted as Team Leader for the Research Team. She is now working again in Westminster for a Conservative MP.

March to April 2009: EHP – the beginning

March 10th was the first full day in the office. It was difficult to know where to start but an action plan and list of tasks seemed like a good idea to provide a structure and get the project started.

The first task was to draft the first leaflet for distribution. I started some work on it and then asked for input and ideas from the others. Thursday was spent going through the leaflet bit by bit with James.

Although this was a time consuming process it was the only way to get it done. I feel that we should test the leaflet out on our target audience before going to print as it is easy for us to understand it as we know what we want it to say but I feel that we need to make sure we do not assume too much with this project and the people we are aiming it at.

Our second pressing task is sorting out the website. We met with Simon the designer and he came up with some great ideas and a fresh new look for both the logo and the website. He is now going to get this up and running. He will also take a look at our leaflet and come up with a vibrant look for this. The design is very important I am positive that this fresh new look will be extremely beneficial to the campaign.

My key priority for this week was to get everything organised and up and running. I set up a spreadsheet with key dates and organised folders on the computer etc, so that we can start as we mean to go on. I felt it would be useful that as a daily task the local and national media was monitored and also the main party websites need regularly checking to keep up with their campaign. I noted that of the three main parties, only the Liberal Democrats had an updated website.

The local Labour party website has not been updated since 2003 and the Conservative website does not seem to have been updated since the last election. I feel that it is essential to keep updating tools such as websites as one reason for voter apathy is the view that parties and candidates only seem to be active during election periods.

If the electorate can see that their representatives are always acting on their behalf and are seen to be working hard then people may be more inclined to partake in politics.

I feel that this is a key point to note and something we really need to think long and hard about following the election in June – how to keep EHP active and in the forefront until the next election and how to keep potential candidates interested and involved.

I am keen to start building links with local media in the coming weeks, but am very cautious not to promote EHP until the website is to a reasonable standard and will attract people in. We are going to take pictures of Hertford to supplement the words on both the leaflet and website.

Livia has started building a ward profile of the key people and organisations we need to know about. This can then be used when we start planning our talks, meetings etc.

I am also keen to set about organising some research which can be conducted to establish why people are apathetic and disillusioned with local politics.

We have our own ideas about why this might be but I am cautious about assuming anything so would like to find out from Hertford locals themselves why they don't bother voting and what they would like to see from their local representatives. What would make them more interested?

I plan to construct a questionnaire which can be put up on the website and then we can analyse the results. I would also like to think about setting up some focus groups and meeting face to face with samples of our target audience. I need to work out how viable this is.

Next week I want to make sure all the old stuff is deleted from the website and we start working on the updates.

Week Two – March 2009

This has been a fairly interesting week. We are finally in the office and getting ourselves settled.

On Wednesday the leaflet came back from Simon, and we are very pleased with his designs. After more proof reading we found a few amendments. It is important to keep checking this through so as to avoid mistakes. We have asked Simon to design us some headed paper and compliments slips too.

April 14th – 17th 2009

This has been a very promising week. It started off with me feeling a tad despondent. The website was up and running, we were on twitter and facebook and we had submitted letters around Hertford and press releases to the media and also the article that Debbie LeMay had written. However we seemed to be getting nowhere. We had also got our blog under way. I am finding this a particularly useful way of getting thoughts down in a bid to prompt debate.

I wasn't sure where to go from here really and then things suddenly picked up. The mercury contacted us saying they were going to run the story by Debbie LeMay and for now would we please partake in their getting to know you column. For this we decide to use Livia as she is the only one from Hertford. Finally some media attention!

This week we also got our fist issue submitted on the website and also had two leaflet replies, a phone call from a businessman in response to a letter who wanted to meet us and a new fan on facebook! Things are looking up.

As a means of provoking further debate I took the initiative to sign East Herts People up to the discover Hertford forums, something I had avoided thus far. I wasn't sure how this would go down with the regular forum contributors but thankfully it has really worked.

We have had some positive and negative response. One guy is persistently trying to dig up some sort of scandal about how we are funded. He managed to unearth Jim's connection and the fact that Jim worked for HSCPM. However this has never been a secret and he thought he was being so clever and had unearthed a potential scandal. I responded with the truth about how we were funded yet this did not seem enough, there's always one!

One recurring theme seems to be that people cannot get their head around the nature of EHP. They want us to have policy and a manifesto and although we have explained that we support and promote Independents this does not seem to be enough. They want to know what we would do about things like Council tax and issues in Bengeo.

I mentioned this to Jim and he reminded me that we do have policy – we promote the idea of community involvement and more participation in local politics. Trying to get across the notion that actual specific policy is down to the individual seems to be an issue with some. My feeling is that this is due to them being desperate for a decent alternative to the current administration!

So forums and blogs aside it has been a very productive week. People are starting to pick up on the idea of EHP. We have sent off a second leaflet draft to Simon and had a draft back from him. The idea is to get this out as soon as possible following in the footsteps off the current leaflet. We want this to be a more specific push for Independents and trying to get across how they are a decent alternative.

This week Jim has voiced the idea of a community newsletter as a long term vision for EHP. These will be tailored for each ward and will feature news, views and info for those who don't really read. It will be short and snappy with a view to promote the website as the place for further information.

This has real potential as local newspapers are struggling and investigative journalism becomes limited. What we need to do is get a design, work on the content and see how people respond to it. We have come up against some protest already as Sele Farm Community centre are worried about impartiality. We may find this with a few places, especially if they are council run.

May - June 2009:

Jim Thornton's Election campaign

Election countdown

From the offset we knew that Jim was going to run in the County Council Elections as a candidate, this was to run alongside the three of us getting EHP going again as a way to raise our profile and encourage others to follow suit.

Election Expenses

Jim was officially made a candidate in the election on May 7th. We wanted to hand his forms in at the last minute as this would give us less time to worry about the regulated period whereby all the money we spend is counted. We worked out that we would have a very small budget. For a local election you are allotted £600 per ward plus 0.05p per elector.

There is a small flaw in this system in the sense that for a Town Council election where you would be standing in one ward you would be allowed this which is fairly generous for such a small scale level of government. For the District it is also the same, fairly justified as District Councillors do make a lot of decisions.

However at County level where you represent a division not just a ward you are severely disadvantaged. A division is made up of two wards. Logic would allow you to assume that this would present a budget of £600x2 plus 0.05p per vote but it does not. The division is not divided up in to individual wards but instead counted as one giant ward so you are given the same budget as Town and District with slightly more money due to the larger number of voters. We knew things were going to be tight.

Designing the Leaflet

The first task was to get Jim's leaflet designed. Jim worked on the wording and I took many action shots of Jim at work. We wanted to go for something different from the other candidates. We wanted something that stood out. We decided that rather than the usual portrait photo and words we would go for a six page DL leaflet and it would feature shots of Jim in action so as to present the idea that Jim would be working on behalf of the local community.

We worked closely with Simon Judd of SJ Creative who had been invaluable in designing our EHP leaflets. No matter what we throw at him he comes back with a great concept and design. We agonised over which shot of Jim to put on the front. Initially I settled for one of him pointing but we decided that gave the wrong impression and was a bit too aggressive. We found a fairly standard shot amidst the array of pictures that we had.

The design that came back was brilliant. It really stood out and we were confident going in to the campaign with this behind us. This did eat quite a large amount of our budget of £1,115, with it costing a hefty £818 but this did include the time spent by the designer and some headed paper that we planned to use as a second leaflet closer to June 4th, we would print these ourselves.

Timesheets

Given Jim's political background and years of experience with the Conservative Party he was a pro at telling me what was required in running the election campaign. We realised that if by some weird twist of fate we were to win this would cause major upset with our opposition and that they would be all over our election expenses looking for mistakes, something that could make our victory void. So we agreed to minimise how much paid time would be spent on Jim's campaign. I constructed timesheets split in to 15 minute intervals so that everything we did could be recorded and traced back.

The Opposition

We knew from the start that our competition was going to be tough. Jim was standing in Hertford St Andrew's where the incumbent was Councillor Peter Ruffles. He is a much loved and well respected local man, born and bred in Hertford and a Councillor on all three levels oh and a friend of Jim's too!

Jim was pretty resigned to the fact he was not going to win and saw the exercise as a means to promote the Independent idea. Peter Ruffles, despite having a very safe seat, was convinced he was going to lose.

When the list of candidates came out, we were up against Ruffles, Tony Bodley of the Labour Party and Sean Shaw of the Liberal Democrat's. Labour is fighting a losing battle in Hertford and the Liberal Democrats are in a pretty similar position. The area is Tory dominated although it has not always been so; it was previously a Labour County Council seat up until 2001 when Peter Ruffles took over from Sir Norman Lindop. We realised we had a good chance of coming second if nothing else.

The first thing to do was get a leaflet designed. Jim decided he wanted something different to the norm where you have a standard leaflet with a mug shot and a bit of writing. He wanted to portray an image of really standing up for people and fighting their corner so we spent about an hour taking lots of action shots of him doing different things, sat at his desk, talking to people etc.

Writing the Manifesto

The manifesto part of the leaflet was up to Jim, he knew the kind of things he wanted to say but was not quite sure how to really portray it. We roughed out some thoughts:

"Election Manifesto – County
You need a fighter to represent you at the County Council
I will fight for <u>you</u> on the County Council: there is no Party telling me how to vote: are you fed up with Tribal Politics?
Photos all 'action' shots: arguing, looking at laptop, round table, looking at bills, outside debating, inspecting
An Independent Councillor can challenge Central Government, and speak out in public and not be muzzled behind closed doors and Challenge waste and unnecessary spending;

How can we get value for money and the best education, environment and community possible?

Jim Thornton believes there is a better way of doing local politics

- *Allowing you to influence your Councillor on line: you help me decide what is best for the Ward: I have no party to tell me how to vote*

- *Using the allowance to pay for Six newsletters a year delivered to your door and maintain the website, a direct phone line during working hours, and somebody to speak to if I am out*

- *Initiatives to establish Ward identity and community: Christian Aid Walk team, sports teams, Quiz Night,*

Specifics:
we need more transparency on spending against budget
Less use of consultants (it is backside covering, and they never get sued when they get it wrong), more use of small local businesses (prequalification and tender lists are not fair)
Bank of Herts
Zero base budgeting
Cut the bureaucracy and push the spending to the front line
In the private sector we ask: how can we get this done? In the public sector they ask: are we allowed to do this?

JDT: civil engineer by profession, runs a family owned group of companies in Hertford involved in Property Management (do not work for local government and do not intend to, refused to be on the Planning Committee); increasing work as an Expert Witness and at Tribunals focussing on accounting issues; governor at Richard Hale and Haileybury; Council of Tyndale House Research Library in Cambridge;

8 years at East Herts fighting behind closed doors; limited success – skate park, cinema, teachers housing, charitable trust (book "Independents for East Herts" later in the summer detailing eight years as a Councillor trying to get things done against the opposition of Council Officers and jealous members of my own party, and what can be done about this sad situation) but now we know the enemy we can get a better idea of how to fight it: "

We went along the "fighting for you" stance and chose a picture that looked strong enough without being too off putting. Simon Judd came back with a superb design yet again, a 6pp DL leaflet with a back panel that could be stuck in someone's window in order to advertise Jim.

From the rough notes we produced the final version:

Will you let me speak out for <u>you</u> at County Hall?

Why do I need somebody to speak out for me?

- If you vote for a Party Candidate, when push comes to shove, who comes first: the voter or the Party? I am an Independent ,so only <u>you</u> can tell me how you want me to vote on issues that affect you.
- There is no transparency at County: the party system means the important debates are all behind closed doors. As an Independent I can speak out without being gagged or shackled by Party Whips.
- The County Council spends £1.2bn and in tight times you need to know that it is being spent well. According to the Audit Commission, its accounting systems are inadequate: it had £28m in Icelandic banks, and £284m of property seems to have gone walkabout which is why the 2008 accounts have still not been signed and are now eight months late. As an Independent, I can speak out on this.
- Education, Adult Services, Care of Children—do you know what is going on? As an Independent I can ask embarrassing questions and speak out to the press and media.

How do I know you will say things I agree with?

- I will tell you what I will say, and you can tell me what you think.
- **How?** Using the Internet and a Ward Newsletter. We have to try using new technology to see if we can get better local politics. I will use my allowance of £9828 per annum as a County Councillor to finance the printing and distribution of a Ward newsletter every two months delivered to your door. My blog will tell you what is going on, my website will tell you what the issues are, and you can email me and tell me what to do, and in turn you can see what other people are telling me to do.
- My difficult job is to listen to as many people as possible and then make a decision on the basis of what is best for the Ward. You will not agree with everything I decide to say, but at least you will have the opportunity to contribute to the debate.

So what do you want to say?

- Obviously I want to argue for tighter scrutiny of the Accounts Department, and I want to see that our money is being spent efficiently. I do this for my own business, and although Local Authority Finance is different, the principles are the same.

- Of course the County Council does many good things well, and I want to support those things and see how they can be done even better.
- I want to argue for initiatives to help retain and create jobs: for example, a local bank like the Bank of Essex that Essex County Council are setting up
- I want to see minimal bureaucracy in Education so that maximum cash can go to the front line teachers and schools.
- I want to see an informed debate about a new Airport in the Thames Estuary that would take pressure off Stanstead
- I believe that loneliness is going to be an increasing problem in society: I want to explore what the County can do to create supportive community in our Wards
- I know how hard it is to get things done, having been elected previously to get a skatepark, cheap housing for teachers, a cinema and a charitable trust for East Herts. I underestimated the opposition from Party colleagues and council officers, but at least I know what the problems are

I think Politicians are sleazy and untrustworthy: why should I trust you?

- None of us are perfect, and we all make mistakes, but I have a track record during my eight years as an East Herts Councillor of standing up to the establishment when things go wrong.
- My wife and I have lived in St Andrews Division for 26 years, my children were educated in local schools, and I am a governor of two of them.
- I am a Reader at St Andrews Church, where I have to preach: if I did not at least try to practice what I preach I would have been thrown out long ago.
- Professionally, I am a Chartered Civil Engineer and Builder, and I do an increasing amount of work as a trusted expert witness.
- I am a Trustee of several charitable trusts, and on the Council of a Research Library in Cambridge.
- I am a local businessman, running a group of companies in Hertford involved in property management.
- I don't take anybody's money, and I pay my own way. At East Herts Council I never claimed expenses, and gave my allowance to charity.

Do you really think you can make a difference?

- I think we can all make a difference if we are determined enough, but it has to be a team effort. We get the politicians we deserve, and if we do not bother to vote, or we do not make demands of our elected representatives, then in one sense we only have ourselves to blame if we get awful politicians.

- We need to find new ways of doing local politics, and I have put my money into East Herts People because I think there are new ways we should be trying.
- But I need your help: I can keep you informed on the issues coming up, but when there is one on which you feel strongly, I need you to look at the arguments on both sides and give me your views.
- There are pressures on all of us, on time, on money, but we live in a community and we have to help each other, if only so that perhaps in our turn when we need help, someone will be there for us. I believe we can find ways to build community, starting with the Ward in which we live, and for which we elect people to represent us.
- What I want to see are more people coming forward who are not tied to a political party, but who are willing to be community leaders in their Ward and to speak out in local Government for the people they represent., and not for a Political Party.
- Change has to start somewhere, and you can start the change by voting for me to speak for you at County Hall, rather than for the Party you might support in a General Election.

"East Herts People promotes Independent Councillors. We do not have a manifesto or agenda, except that party politics has no place in local government. We support candidates that have an ear to local people, not Westminster party politics"

Delivering the Leaflets

Partly using information I had drawn up from the previous deliveries of the EHP leaflet and partly using Jim's expertise we drew up a concise strategy of how to deliver Jim's leaflets as quickly as possible because we wanted to hit people before the postal votes came out and then we wanted there to be a second leaflet targeted at key areas in the immediate run up to the election.

Blocks of flats proved a problem, you had to get in early to use the tradesman's entrance. Mitre Court proved particularly difficult with Livia getting stuck in there on one occasion due to the highly secure nature of it. Jim spent some time analysing the streets and the number of houses etc and divided the polling districts up in to smaller segments so that the prospect of leaflet delivery was not quite as frightening. Luckily Jim had some volunteers from the last election who were supporters of the Independent campaign.

For two weeks Jim pounded the streets with his leaflets, seemingly breaking records with his delivery times! I did some in the evenings on my way home and discovered it was a fairly pleasant activity. One thing that did start to grate was the inadequacy of many letter boxes. The ones with the draft extractor brush type mechanisms often resulted in far too much hand going through the letter box in order to get the leaflets through!

Issues

Jim thought he had struck gold when early in to his campaign he discovered the Richard Hale Sports hall issue. Being a governor of the school Jim was present at a meeting when it emerged that there was some controversy over a planned sports hall for the school. The sports hall had planning permission granted 5 years ago and it was planned that it would be a community sports hall which would benefit Hertford.

However it had not received the funding from the County Council that it required. Meanwhile Presdales School in Ware had received funding and did not even have planning permission.

Even more interestingly, Peter Ruffles was a governor for the school. So, Jim wanted to know why Peter had not fought Richard Hale's corner given the fact it was a school in his division yet he had supported the Presdales cause because he was a Governor. Jim started to use this as an issue for his second leaflet and we set about promoting the issue.

However half way through Jim started to doubt his tactics, the Richard Hale issue had the potential to alienate Sele residents and those parents who sent their children to school at Presdales as many do. He thought about maybe posting these sheets around areas close to the school but long gone are the days whereby children go to school on their doorstep.

After much debate the issue was pushed aside and we went back to focussing on three good reasons why we should vote for Jim and printing maps of how to get to the polling stations.

Market stall

One election tactic was to pay the £25 to EHDC to have a stall in Hertford Market on a Saturday. We did one three weeks before the election and it was a great way for Jim to be seen and for EHP to have a presence. The stall consisted of Jim's leaflets and a bit of EHP information. We had some stands and an umbrella and it was a great way for people just to see what we were about. The response rate was encouraging, a few people came over to chat and ask Jim questions.

Of course inevitably you get a lot of nutters for want of a better word. A particular favourite of mine was the lady who came over and ranted at me about the state of Broxbourne and then ranted on about the way the government were abusing bee keepers and the danger that bee's were in. Great stuff! I also had to appease a racist old lady without offending her "I said to a policeman the other day that the best way to treat those immigrants that commit crime is to send them back to their country, that'll teach them". To which I smiled politely and told her to use her vote! Mostly these people just want to get something off their chest.

The following week Jim decided to cut out the expense of a market stall and after gaining permission from the Council he just handed some leaflets out in town on a Saturday. During all of this, Jim did get a very favourable response from people. There seemed to be an underlying current that there was room for change and maybe Independent's could provide this.

MPs Expenses

Something unprecedented happened in May that could not have been more perfect for EHP, for Jim and for Independent's in general. The MP's expenses scandal had been rumbling along for a while now ever since the Derek Conway affair in 2008. In May 2009, The Daily Telegraph revealed the true extent of the scandal and for weeks kept unearthing more and more facts about where exactly our tax payer's money was being spent. Some of the classic examples included moat maintenance and payment for a duck house.

These revelations led to a public outcry about the state of our politicians and apathy and disillusionment hit an all time high. People began talking about alternatives to the current system and more and more the word Independent kept being used. Perhaps independently elected representatives were the way forward, people who could not hide behind their party and were accountable directly to the electorate.

Newspaper articles were being written about it, endless editorials were constructed and a few celebrities came out of the woodwork claiming they would rise up against our crooked MP's and represent the people the most high profile being Esther Rantzen although there was hope that Martin Bell might consider standing again.

This was perfect for us. We could present ourselves as anti-sleaze, free of scandal. We were up against a Conservative, traditionally known for their excessive and scandalous ways (Although not so much Peter Ruffles it must be said!) At one of the market stalls we mentioned politician's expenses and the mood on the street was that people were fed up. Mostly they did not really understand the issue. They tarred all representatives with the same brush. However if this didn't help us win some votes then nothing would!

Communications and Blogging

We used the EHP website to promote Jim. He had his own page and also we encouraged him to contribute to the blog and we later discovered that a good few people were following this.

In the lead up to June 4th we did as much as we could with such short time, small support and limited resources. We heard form a lot of people that our leaflet was certainly the best. Peter Ruffles had a side on the Conservative newsletter, Labour produced a generic county wide leaflet and there was nothing from the Lib Dem who was clearly a paper candidate. We went in to June 4th feeling confident and slightly optimistic.

Election Day:

Livia has written up the election day in her Diary, but these are the key points I noted down:

- Lack of effort from other parties
- Slow turnout in the morning and right up through the day

- Really doubted any success for JT prior to the afternoon
- By the evening I was feeling more hopeful, I think we may have a genuine chance.
- Loud hailer – embarrassing to start off with but really got in to it by the end.
- Telling is a useful way of gauging turnout
- People are friendly
- Important to maintain a presence and grab attention
- Seems to be a feeling that people want change, I think it will be tight.
- Looked after a dog to assist a voter!

June and July 2009

Hertford Town Council By-Elections

In May we were informed that there were to be two vacancies on the town council. One councillor was retiring but there seemed to be an underlying reason why he was doing this now, something to do with council decisions particularly at Sele Farm. The other councillor had been thrown out for his lack of attendance at meetings.

We noticed the vacancies through an article in The Mercury and soon realised we needed to request a by-election. If we didn't, the majority party could simply fill the vacancies in house, the majority party being the Tory party.

This did not seem democratically right to us and also it seemed a blessing to be given a further opportunity though which to further promote the Independent cause. We rallied our signatures; first for Sele and then for Castle, ten were needed for each. We submitted them in time.

East Herts District Council

It soon became clear that we were not EHDC's favourite people, and this was confirmed further upon submission of the signatures.

One conversation with an employee of the electoral office astounded me as I was told that it was basically a huge inconvenience that we had requested the by-election as they had enough to worry about in respect of the June 4th County and European elections.

I was undeterred however, it was the electorate's right to hold an election. Jenny Watson the new Chair of the Electoral Commission summed up the point of elections superbly in her inaugural speech recently; *"I think too many of us forget who, exactly, elections are there to benefit. We forget that they're not aimed at helping governments, or parties, or individual candidates. They're there for voters. To give them a voice."*

This is exactly the point we were trying to prove. Yes we were hoping to further our own cause but it is all interlinked. We want people to have more choice in local politics. Local government in Hertfordshire is consistently dominated by one party and particularly in Hertford there is little choice for the electorate,

Labour and the Liberal Democrats have all but given up in the town as they are aware their core support is not enough to make any impact. This is due to that age old problem of people tactically voting or not voting at all through disillusionment or resignation to the fact that the Conservatives are going to win.

So, by ensuring that a by-election was to be held we were giving the decision making process rightfully back to the electorate. Elected representatives no matter how minor are there to represent us and we should make the most of the fact that in this country we are able to have our say. So many people are in the position whereby they have no choice or say over who represents them, and often even if they do, they have little choice but to vote in accordance with the wishes of their leader.

My run in with EHDC left me feeling somewhat disheartened with their attitude. To a 9-5 worker it may not be important to hold an election because it involves too much paperwork but we owe it to those less privileged than ourselves to make the most of our voting responsibilities.

Finding the candidates

Alongside the promotion and running of Jim's campaign for office we had the daunting task of finding candidates for the by-election. We wanted fresh faces, people who were new to politics but had ideas, people who wanted to represent their community free of party governance, who could answer solely to local people. However, how were we going to find them?

Initially I had scouted someone out from the Discover Hertford forum, I invited them in for an interview, explained the role and tried not to put any pressure on them to decide, I wanted it to be very much their decision. Unfortunately it seemed this was not really a good time for them to take on something like this.

Next we tried someone that Jim knew who was interested in standing in Sele, she spent a long time deliberating and discussing with her family but unfortunately this was not a good time for her and she did not want to enter in to this without being fully committed. You cannot argue with this. There is a real danger that if you force someone or put pressure on them they become simply a paper candidate with no real drive to be standing as a representative. We really needed people to come to us.

The next idea I had was an advert in the paper, simply advertising for potential candidates. Jim decided this was certainly worth trying. To coincide with this we drew up a detailed guide to how to be a councillor. The idea was that we would advertise the role, and ask people to request an information pack for further consideration. This was not cheap; an advert in the paper was going to cost around £400 for one week. It did attract some response though. People contacted us and requested an information pack.

It was not until June 4th (Election Day) that we heard when the by-elections might be held. The rumour was July 21st. A couple of our enquiries seemed quite keen to see the Town Council election through. One guy called up on the day that the advert went out and said he was keen to stand in the by-election and was keen to stand as an Independent, he had already contacted the council and found out the details and they had told him about us.

I asked him if he could come in and meet with me. He agreed. However, what ensued was a series of cancelled appointments, large amounts of rescheduling and also times when he just didn't show up at all.

At first this was fine, I realised he was busy and worked in London but then we discovered the official notice had been posted announcing the election, we had a week to get two candidates and submit their signed forms.

I contacted him again and eventually got through to him. He told me he was now unable to stand in the election as he did not have the time. I told him to get in touch in time for the District elections should he be interested then. I thought that was the end of it.......

I was in contact with a guy called James Morris throughout June who expressed a strong interest to stand as a candidate. I met with him and he decided he definitely wanted to do it. Although he was relatively new to Hertford having only lived here for three years or so, he was keen, eager and intelligent and seemed to have a genuine interest in making a difference and representing people as an Independent.

So this was the candidate for Castle. Sele was proving slightly trickier. Four days before the deadline I still had no candidate, I was beginning to give up hope. A few weeks previously I had been contacted by a lady who surprisingly had been forwarded our details by a Conservative Councillor. She did not seem overly political but was keen to stand and represent the people of Sele. In the run up to the deadline I had no luck getting hold of her so assumed she had lost interest.

However, on the Monday, two days before the nomination deadline she rang us back. She was still keen. Talk about working to the wire. She came in the next day and we went through her forms. We now had our two candidates.

On the Wednesday we had until 12pm to submit the forms. James kindly volunteered to drive the forms to Bishop's Stortford, our only hope of getting them in on time.

At 11.30am he returned with two forms declaring the successful nomination of Angela Emsley and James Morris as Independent candidates for the by-election. We had done it by the skin of our teeth.

Who do we support and why?

One of the problems we faced was how to decide who could stand and who we would represent. I identified this problem fairly early on; it seemed like a flaw in the otherwise fairly straightforward EHP plan.

Elections cost money, and someone has to provide that money. Of course you are allowed to do this yourself, as you probably would need to if you wanted to run independently but realistically how many people have a spare grand knocking about for those times when you want to represent your community?

The answer is of course relatively few. Luckily for EHP Jim is prepared to invest his own hard earned money in to this cause and EHP supported Independent candidates are able to rely on support both financially and practically from Jim. However, here is the problem: Independents are representatives who are not affiliated to a political party; theoretically anyone can run as an Independent as long as they are over 18 and not a criminal (alongside a few other prerequisites).

However, there is a trend that minor; fringe and Independent parties can attract extreme views simply because none of the mainstream parties will have them. This is of course a huge sweeping generalisation, but it was a factor that we needed to take in to account. How were we going to regulate the candidates without going against the basic EHP principles?

The Jury Team

We had observed the workings of the Jury Team, who emerged in March 2009. The way I can best describe them is a national version of EHP! They were founded by Sir Paul Judge, a former Tory. His mantra was "Politics without Parties", similar to our own view of "People not Parties".

Their launch in March received a large amount of publicity and media coverage, it was all rather interesting to observe. Their aim was to find and promote Independent candidates for the June 4th European Elections with a view to provide a full range of candidates at the General

Election in 2010. I followed their emergence with intrigue and also with hope that maybe we could borrow a few ideas from them.

One thing I did like was their way of selecting candidates, an area I felt needed more work as far as EHP were concerned. People could sign up as members of the Jury Team and then people could also nominate themselves as candidates if they wanted to. The final list of candidates was chosen after a vote conducted through a text message system whereby all of the members had the right to choose who would stand.

I really liked this idea and due to the large amount of coverage they received they were able to gather quite a lot of membership which meant there was a fairly democratic process involved in choosing the candidates.

I thought that maybe in the future we should try something similar, a way of attracting signed up members (not necessarily paid ones, just subscribers) and allow them to choose from a list of nominated candidates.

What about this idea?

The Conservatives announced on Friday July 10th their intention to hold an open primary in Totnes in order to select a candidate for Parliament to replace Anthony Steen. This is a huge step forward for democracy and electorate participation in the UK. Every voter in Totnes will receive a ballot paper and be able to choose from a list of candidates. Local party members have already chosen a short list of 11 candidates and the voters will then narrow this down to the final choice; who will then stand in the general election.

This is a great way to engage with the voter and I really think this is important. Times are changing and we need to find ways to re-engage with the electorate who are increasingly more disillusioned with the political system. I think EHP can build on both this and the Jury Team idea.

If we go back to basics, build up local support, encourage people to nominate themselves as candidates and then use either the internet or maybe a public ballot to enable local people to choose who represents them on a local level. This would really allow us to take it back to the grassroots. We want to encourage Independent voices to stand up and represent their community and we should allow the community to choose these voices.

Vitruvius

The reason for mentioning the above information is that we faced the problem of who to support/how we decided, earlier than anticipated when the issue of the Town Council by-election came to the forefront. Vitruvius (not his real name) was a former candidate for EHP in 2007 who was still keen to fly the Independent flag. He was hopeful he could run as an Independent in the by-election.

Jim had contacted him during his campaign in regard to leafleting and the by-election had been mentioned. However Jim had said from the beginning that he was not sure this guy was the right person to fly the Independent flag on behalf of EHP.

I had been in contact with him from an early stage and had found him quite frustrating, trying to tell us how to do things; my particular favourite was his insistence on telling us (a group of researchers in our very early twenties) how to engage with the youth of today. Without wanting to sound ageist, this guy is mid fifties!

So, after much deliberation we decided he wasn't the sort of person we wanted to put EHP money behind. This was a tricky and controversial issue but at the end of the day it was Jim's money that was behind EHP and it seemed it may be a waste of all our hard work to back a loose cannon of a candidate.

The problem with Vitruvius was certainly not his enthusiasm, this was flowing. The problem was mainly his inability to grasp basic information and concepts and his ability to rile people very easily. Once we knew the by-election was here we had to tell him that unfortunately we would not be able to back him financially but obviously we could not stop him running as an Independent and we wished him all the best.

His immediate response was to field himself as a candidate for Castle and to persuade his friend, Rosie, to stand in Sele. He was determined to fight this. Straight away he proved why we should not back him financially when he insisted that Jim was lying about having funded the

2007 campaign and claimed that election expenditure could be claimed back from the council – not true!

Jim offered him our support in other ways with election boundaries, maps and street and voter analysis. We also gave him the relevant forms that he needed. At one point I thought he wouldn't even get the forms in on time because he was insistent that the forms could be handed in to the Hertford Council offices as opposed to the Bishops Stortford offices!

Obviously, it was not an ideal situation to be placed in to have two Independents in each ward fighting it out, well this was how I perceived it, but Jim put a positive spin on it that this was what EHP was all about, more choice and more candidates to stand up against the continual dominance of one party.

Vitruvius did attempt a bargain at one point by offering us the option of his Sele candidate standing down if our Castle candidate stood down but we informed him that this was not an option. The point of Independents is that anyone can stand and there is no limit on candidates.

You do have the danger that perhaps more than one Independent will split the anti Tory vote but you have the plus of giving people more choice which I believe democratically is what it should be about. After all, there are so many nations where they do not have the privilege of voting.

The Opposition Candidates

Without us bargaining anything the mysterious Rosie was soon removed from the list in Hertford Sele which left Angela to fight it out against the Tory candidate Darren Ypey. This was when I began to realise we might have a genuine chance.

Darren Ypey was a shock choice of candidate when the nominations were revealed, as he had previously been in contact with me in response to my advert in the Mercury asking for candidates. He seemed really keen and eager to stand as an Independent and had done his research.

When it came to nomination time he proved fairly elusive to track down and kept agreeing to come in and meet with me and then cancelling/not turning up. With a few days to go before the nomination papers were due in I called him and asked him if he was still interested to which he replied that he was not in a position to stand at this election as he did not have the time so I told him to get back in touch in a couple of years in time for the District elections.

I thought that was the end of it but then he was revealed as the Conservative candidate for Sele. I would like to point out that there is no problem with this, it is great that he wanted to stand at all and if he believed that standing for a party was the best option then that is perfectly acceptable.

However I did not appreciate the underhand manner and would have appreciated an honest response rather than being endlessly messed about. Perhaps he was embarrassed, who knows? However he should have realised that it would have come out sooner or later. Honesty really is the best policy!

When the list of nominations was published we found out it was us versus the Tories along with Vitruvius to add to the equation in Castle. The Tory candidate in Sele was the elusive Darren Ypey whilst the Castle candidate was a young chap (23) called Matthew McCormick.

The Campaign

Following the near success of Jim's campaign we felt confident in running the by-election campaign. We got Simon Judd in again to do the leaflets and yet again he came back with two superb designs.

I decided that the two leaflets should be different designs to reflect the difference in the candidates and also to counteract any comments about EHP being a party or the Independents being the same. Independents should be identified on an individual basis. So we agreed the designs, the candidates constructed the content with some guidance from myself and then we sent them to print.

The leaflets were key to this campaign. They needed to be eye catching and to the point. Often with these things that you put through the door you have a matter of seconds to grab the recipient's attention before they end up in the bin.

The way I perceived the candidates was that James would appeal because he is young and ambitious and fresh whilst Angela would appeal because she is down to earth, honest and different to the norm. Sele would be a very good place to try and encourage votes for Angela whilst Castle would be tough but not impossible.

Leaflet delivery is always a tiring job and no mean feat for a person on their own so I was determined that Angela and James, although inevitably having to do a lot of the hard work themselves, would be able to rely on some support along the way. I do not have an aversion to the odd round of leaflet delivery and neither does Jim. Conveniently we were able to use some of our budget to pay for leaflet delivery too. James and Angela would certainly have their work cut out though.

Luckily we still had all of the network plans from both Jim's campaign and the community newsletters. Although at the time this took up a lot of effort it has been an invaluable tool that will serves us well although I anticipate that it will require updating as and when the electoral roll/census is updated.

The EHP website has been a further invaluable tool by which to advertise the election and feature information on the candidates. We also encouraged the candidates to contribute blog entries. James was keen for this but Angela was not so which was fine, it is not for everyone. James kept a blog charting his campaign.

Both Angela and James set up email addresses for each ward so that people could contact them with any questions they might have. It is essential that you have some internet presences nowadays and I really do feel our campaign was strengthened by the ability for people to read about the candidates on our website. We also have 200 odd followers on twitter and regular 'tweets' about the goings on of the election campaign were important.

Campaigning in the Market

The Saturday before the election I accompanied James and Angela in to town to hand out leaflets in the market. The Conservatives had a stall outside the book shop but neither of the candidate's were present, just the usual suspects and not many people were talking to them.

We stood some distance away and spoke to a few people. I really do feel that the most important thing when running for any type of political office is to be seen and to meet as many people as possible. The old fashioned way is the best way, people are much more likely to consider voting for you if they have met you or at the very least seen you.

As for the other candidates, not once did we see a leaflet for Darren Ypey. To the contrary the Conservatives really seemed to be pushing Matthew McCormick's candidacy in Hertford Castle. I believe that perhaps they knew they had more of a chance in Castle.

Sele is traditionally Labour and Angela stood a good chance. Matthew McCormick's first leaflet was soon delivered and interestingly was endorsed by Councillor Peter Ruffles. The Tories then delivered a second leaflet fairly swiftly to ensure maximum impact.

We did not hear anything from Vitruvius until the week before the election where out of nowhere he produced a rather fancy looking postcard/leaflet and set up a myspace page. It was good to see that the candidates were taking this seriously and the Tories in particular were not resting on their laurels.

One thing that was for certain was that the by-election had allowed for a really good election campaign with each side needing to make sure they pulled out all the stops. This was both good for Hertford and good for local democracy.

Getting out the Voters

The main problem with the by-election was going to be attracting the voters. The benefit of the June 4th election was that it was a nationwide event, attracting extensive media coverage. This was a local by-election for the town council which was rather bizarrely being held on a Tuesday not a Thursday.

So the change of day was against us and there was very little media coverage with the Mercury running a couple of token pieces. Friday's edition before the election contained a small article in a side column which could be easily overlooked. We were up against it. The only thing we could rely on were the organised people who would receive their polling card and make a note of the day, the postal voters and the few who took a real interest in local politics.

This is one area that really needs to be addressed. How do we maximise the awareness of local elections and encourage people to vote? The internet is one thing but more needs to be done. Local media, particularly in Hertford is scarce and unreliable. The main newspaper 'The Mercury' is not particularly political and is also declining in readership, as are many other local newspapers.

Other than the Mercury you have local radio which is Hertfordshire wide and not specific to Hertford itself, a couple of other free papers but all in all a pretty poor show. There is a fairly active website called *Discover Hertford* but that is only really used by a select few. It is difficult to really spread the word, that is why leaflets and door to door is best,

A Curious Letter

Media coverage in the Mercury was not extensive. Between the 24th June and the 24th July it consisted of three articles and a letter. Two of the articles highlighting that there was going to be a by-election, one reporting the results and the letter was about the lack of involvement from all the parties/disappointing response rate.

This letter was very mysterious. It was from a man named Colin Sussex and said the address has been supplied. The reason it was suspicious was that it was heavily in favour of Independents over parties. It highlighted the fact Labour and the Lib Dem's had no candidates and pointed out the shoddy record of Sacha Bright's attendance expressing that perhaps the Conservatives weren't right for the job. The underlying theme was the necessity for the by-election to take place in order to ensure people had their say. It mentioned Independent's as the only real alternative and mentioned Vitruvius personally commenting that he had no idea who James Morris even was.

Mr Sussex also conveniently knew about Rosie's decision to step down, something I was not aware was public knowledge. I looked Mr Sussex up on the electoral roll as I figured he was probably a good person for James to go and visit but rather bizarrely there was no one by that name on there. This was odd considering Mr Sussex's extensive knowledge of the electoral process in Hertford and it seemed odd that someone from outside the wards would be that bothered by the event.

It was then that I began to suspect something was amiss. If I am honest, straight off the letter smacked of Vitruvius. There was too much knowledge of the Independents and it all seemed a bit convenient that this person was a friend of Vitruvius. At the very least he must have put someone up to it, the clincher was the use of an inverted comma to highlight a word, something Vitruvius is rather partial to, having experienced many of his emails.

I raised my suspicions to Jim, Livia and James and I am not sure anyone thought it possible. However, James went to the Duncombe Arms on the Saturday before the by-election and spoke to Vitruvius, questioning him about the letter and asking why Colin Sussex didn't seem to exist. He admitted rather sheepishly that it might have been him. I thought as much!

The Final Days

The final few days up to the election involved a final round of leaflet delivery, handing out leaflets in town/talking to the public and leafleting the train stations.

Saturday in town was interesting, the Conservatives had a market stall which was manned by the usual suspects, no sign of the actual candidates and the response we got from the public ranged from supportive, to indifferent to slightly abusive ("I'm not going to vote for any crooks"?!) Angela found this a bit much as she maintains she is an honest candidate.

The unfortunate thing is that so few people really understand politics and the way it works that they cannot comprehend what you are trying to do. The MP's expenses scandal seems to have tarred anyone vaguely involved in politics with the same brush.

Leafleting the train stations is always fun, I am never sure how successful it is. We focused on Hertford North because that is where most people come in. The trouble with it is that we cannot be sure where people live and with two candidates in two different areas, it is hard to know which leaflet to give them, so we settled for both.

Election Day

The day of the election was a quiet affair, not surprisingly the turnout was 14.1% for Sele and 14.3% for Castle. By-elections are notoriously low in turnout and even more so for a local level election. There was little advertisement and a large amount of apathy and disillusionment.

The Count was held in Castle Hall and we soon learnt that Angela had beaten Darren Ypey of the Conservatives when we saw the proportion of her votes to his during the verification. Soon enough Angela was declared the winner, winning by a comfortable 334 to 264 votes.

On the Castle count table it was a slightly more nail biting situation. James was fending off competition from both Vitruvius and Matthew McCormick. Matthew's pile was increasing rapidly, and we could see it was a clear Tory win. The worry came from the question of whether in the end Vitruvius's and James's votes would combine to actually beat the Tory votes thus meaning that we had properly split the anti-Tory vote.

However in the end James came second and combined with Vitruvius the votes did not quite match those of Matthew. Matthew won 471 to 222 to 190.

So all in all, a fairly rewarding evening, we were so pleased for Angela, who looked genuinely thrilled to have been elected.

I was disappointed for James because I felt he was a strong and passionate candidate who would have made an excellent Councillor but he remained stoic and resilient and vowed to come back and fight for a seat on the District Council in 2011.

After nearly five months of tireless campaigning and building up the EHP name we had an elected Independent representative.

We had proved we were a force to be reckoned with, one that could win elections.

Analysis

In total, the number of votes cast for Independents was slightly more than the total votes cast for the Conservatives. This is so encouraging. We are slowly ingratiating ourselves in to the publics favour. In Castle we knew we had a fight on our hands, it is quite a Tory area but Matthew McCormick did not win that convincingly considering the nature of the seat.

This by-election shows us that there is definite potential to keep up the EHP fight and plough on to 2011 where potentially we could really make some changes to local government in East Herts. Angela's win has proved this and we now have to find ways to engage further with the electorate, keep the momentum going and persuade others to follow in her footsteps and represent their local community.

Ideas for the future

How to continue what we have started; promote EHP even further; expand it through East Herts and provide a full list of candidates for 2011:

Use of the Internet

Much more needs to be made of the Internet in local elections. I would like to see a dedicated person within the EHDC electoral office working solely on internet communications in the run up to the election. There is information on the EHDC website but it is not enough and is not updated enough.

Why can't we have an impartial site that tells us who the candidates for each ward and division are, giving people the chance to read about their candidates and make an informed choice? There is so much scope for promotion of elections through the Internet and this is an area that is being completely overlooked.

I monitored the websites of the three main parties prior to and during the election period. Hertfordshire Lib Dems had the most active website. The Conservative website was not easy to access; it was only through my searching that I came across the relevant one for County level and it was not very well set up. However to its credit it did include information about each of the councillors and the generic Tory manifesto for County Hall.

Labour's website had not been updated since 2003, aside from the odd newsletter that had been uploaded. Information on the candidates was near on impossible to locate and the only leaflet we encountered was a generic

Social Networking

Twitter may just be a phase or a fad but it is a highly effective one at that. These things have to be explored and Twitter has proved to be a very useful way of promoting

Ideas:

- Youth forum

- Focus groups as a form of market research to find out the issues that are important to 18-35 year olds and what they want local councillors to focus on.

- If Jim was to be elected then ideally a full time webmaster would be required to keep updating the website.

- Drop in sessions where people can be part of the decision making process, and regular news updates.

- Create opportunities for open debates with other councillors.

- Public meetings where people can air their views. Print lists of upcoming meetings and distribute these.

- Mailing lists for different issues to keep certain people informed about issues relevant to them so as not to bombard people with unwanted information.

- For blogs, we all need to contribute to these. Twitter is definitely effective, far more effective for businesses, politicians and those promoting things, this is what people want to read.

- Public debates in run up to election are a must – can officially use rooms during designated periods.

- First delivery is key – needs to be informative, up to date and relevant.

Appendix 3
Livia's Diary

Livia Oldland read Theology & Religious Studies at the University of Leeds. She has done part-time casework for a Liberal Democrat MP, and an internship with think tank Theos. She worked part-time for East Herts People from March to October 2009, and now works for the Independent Network, providing support to Independent Parliamentary Candidates.

1st April 2009

I Worked on 'Guide to being a Councillor' for EHP website, e-mailed Herts Direct for East Herts People to be put on their website, and did some Media Monitoring.

All three of us went and distributed leaflets and postcards around shops and businesses in Hertford in the afternoon. I was most successful with hairdressers, beauticians, pubs and cafes, accepting most leaflets.

Many shops were not willing to display our leaflets or postcards as they were concerned that it would be offensive to members of the public with other political allegiances, this was especially true of the hairdressers Fringe Benefits. I personally don't see how our leaflets and postcards could offend anyone; we are not members of the BNP! It seems that in today's society, you are only allowed to hold private political views and you should not discuss them in public.

Also Hertford Library and the Local Tourist Office refused to display our leaflet/poster as it was against their rules to display any political material. This was disappointing for us, since the notice boards in Hertford library are read by many and contain community events and clubs. This only reiterated my point that you could only be politically active in private, definitely not in a library! I found it disturbing that politics was being removed so much from public life. Surely politics is about being an active citizen and therefore its rightful place should be in places of a community, such as a library or tourist centre.

3rd April 2009

-Completed 'Guide to being a Councillor' for EHP Website. I really enjoyed doing this and hope it will be beneficial for future candidates.

-Produced mail merge letter for charity

-Worked on draft of 2nd leaflet

8th April 2009

-All the team had a meeting with Debbie LeMay, Independent Councillor for Buntingford. From the meeting she was able to write a press release for us, which was sent to Herts Mercury. The article focused on East Herts People trying to get young people to vote.

From the meeting I produced 'An interview with Debbie LeMay, to put on the website'-Laura contributed to this as well.

It was great to met Debbie LeMay, as she truly is an inspirational Councillor and obviously enjoys her public role. If only we could encourage others to stand as Independent Councillors?

-I also worked again on draft of 2nd leaflet

-Wrote an issues page on a new waste treatment plant to be built in Hatfield area. They plan to recover energy from burning waste. Herts County Council argues that this is an effective measure to reduce landfill, but why can't we recycle the waste and encourage less packaging from manufactories?

9th April 2009

-Emailed contacts for Youth Parliament and East Herts Council. For Youth Parliament, asked regional coordinator, if I could have contact details of Hertford and the surrounding areas MYP and asked their advice for engaging younger people in politics. I contacted East Herts Council to ask for the contact details of youth councillors and methods they have found useful of involving young people in politics.

-Produced mail merge letter to charities and churches, explaining who were are and the need for independents, over 50 letters sent.

-Sorted out leaflets to be distributed.

-Wrote another draft for second leaflet.

-Emailed hertford.net to be put on their contacts list.

-Emailed religious institutions, which we only had one email address for.

Monday 20th April 2009

-Uploaded Debbie LeMay article to website

-Produced letters to local governors

-Wrote blog entry

-Did news article on gypsies
There are current plans to allocate land for gypsy site. I wrote an article on the proposed plans, but Laura felt the article was too controversial and the article was never published.

Wednesday 22nd April 2009

Mr Peter Ruffles came into our office in the morning for a very pleasant chat, it is very unusual for a member of the opposition to come into office and speak with us openly.

Mr Ruffles mentioned to us that he was going to the opening ceremony of a Mind Centre held at Castle Hall, the Celebrity guest was Alistair Campbell. Of course, all of us jumped at the chance at going to meet Alistair Campbell.

We all went to the opening ceremony for the new Mind centre in Castle Hall for around an hour and half during lunch time. At the event, Peter Ruffles spoke as he was deputy mayor and Mr Campbell spoke about his battle with mental illness. Mr Campbell gave a very interesting and inspiring speech, it was great to hear a politician openly admit to suffering from a mental illness. I can only wish that more did.

After Mr Campbell's speech he read an excerpt from his book, which was very interesting. We also had a talk on the benefits of Cognitive Behavioral Therapy (CBT) from a Professor at the University of Hertfordshire, I certainly felt like I had learnt a lot from his talk.

-Researched environmental issues for East Herts

-Researched local events in Hertford in the next few months

Friday 24th April 2009

-Completed research on environment in East Herts.

-Media monitoring

-Sent form to council regarding license of distribution of free literature

Unfortunately you need a license from the council to hand out leaflets in public property. We needed this license so we could hand out our postcard/leaflet to members of the public in Hertford Town Centre. The form to fill out was relatively easy, but cost £20, I think it is ridiculous that you have to apply for a license to hand out leaflets and is just an example of too much bureaucracy!

Wednesday 29th April 2009

In the evening I attended the Annual Town Council meeting held at Hertford Castle. During the event there were presentations for Herts County Council on the local library services, local allotment group, Hertford Museum, Hertford Fair Trade and a round-up of what Hertford Town Council has been up to during the last 3 months. All the presentations were very interesting.

During the evening I also spoke to Richard West of the Fair Trade group and councillors including Hilary Durbin who was extremely pleasant. She spoke to me about the Fair Trade Group which she is an active member and also the problems she experiences as being the only Labour Councillor on the Town Council. From speaking with her, it was evident that tribal politics existed on the Town Council and was affecting decision making and the cohesive structure of the council.

Labour activist Tony Bodley was also present at the meeting. At the Q&A session Tony Bodley aggressively accused the Hertford Town Council meeting of not doing enough to stop the motorcyclists in Archers Spring; he also presented a petition on Archers Spring. This led to a heated debate between Tony Bodley and councillors on Hertford Town Council.

May 2009 Diary

As we started the month we entered the nomination period for Jim's election campaign and had to adhere to keeping a strict timesheet. Even though this was quite annoying it was essential to monitor electoral expenditure and to ensure that we did not go over budget.

May 4tt–May 8th 2009

During the week I was responsible for designing a pull-up display that could be used by EHP at public events. The design had to be generic as it was planned to be used far in the future.

We decided to go for two pull-up display stands from Prontoprint. It was quite hard difficult to design, since this was the first time I had ever properly designed anything since school and we only had published.

In the end I decided to go with the first display stand having our logo and a simple slogan. For the second display I decided to do a table on what the responsibilities are for each level of council.

The display was finished on Friday and I thought that they looked excellent, especially the display with information on Council duties.

I also spent some time on Friday handing out EHP leaflets to members of the public in Hertford Town Centre. Even though this was quite embarrassing, I think it was important to maintain a public profile. I bumped into Cllr Mike Tindale who spoke to me about how East Herts People were doing and our recent successes, unfortunately I feel that he may have been sarcastic!

Monday 11th-15th May 2009

As we still had a valid license, I spent part of Monday morning handing our leaflets again in the Town

27th May 2009

The start of the week has proven to be really exciting. Laura has organised an advert to be published in the local Mercury, asking local people to get involved with local government and stand as Independent Councillors. Hopefully within the next few weeks we should get responses back from people who would like to stand as Independent Councillors. As we have two by-elections in Hertford Town Council coming up in the next few months, we desperately need people to stand as Independent Councillors

The MPs' expenses story has been fueling the media for the last month or so and it has been free publicity for the Independents. It was fantastic to see that Esther Ranzen and Martin Bell would like to stand as Independent Prospective Parliament Candidate. The media has been rife with articles on Independents in Councillors. Not all media interest has been positive, since many comment sections have noted that parliament wouldn't work with non-aligned MPs. Unfortunately there has been hardly any media interest on Independent Councillors, which is surprising since there is an election coming up.

Today I have spent compiling the 'Guide to being an Independent County Council'. Is all interesting stuff, had one hic up as the server went down and I lost all my work. Hopefully this will be done in the next few days.

East Herts People is trying to encourage people to vote next week and to stop voter apathy. To do this, I have applied for a license from East Herts Council to distribute leaflets/postcards in Hertford next week.

Jim's campaign is on full steam ahead and he has been busy distributing his second leaflet all around Hertford. The current gossip is that Jim stands a good chance, we will find out next week if this is correct.

Interestingly local media on local councillors hasn't been too positive recently. The Mercury reported last Friday (22nd May) that Cllr Tindale was trying to stop Cllrs Nigel and Deborah Clark from raising questions in meetings. This was overturned and was not good publicity for Cllr Tindale. Also East Herts Election Office at East Herts Council sent a polling card to a 16yr old, who turned out to be a MYP. Again, we will find out next week, if this affects the election.

Election Week

Monday

On Monday I went into town during the morning and afternoon for several hours promoting East Herts People. I wore the fabulous East Herts People t-shirt and gave out East Herts People leaflets and postcards. The people of Hertford were quite friendly and receptive, many people took a leaflet and some stopped to talk about East Herts People and Jim Thornton. Even more encouraging was that some local people stated that they were going to vote for Jim.

On Monday I also spent time amending the banner for East Herts People. The banner was general advertising for East Herts People and was very large at over 3 meters long. But unfortunately the banner stated the previous district council elections date on it and needed to be changed. I eventually found a shop in Hertford that would amend the banner for ten pounds. The banner was displayed on Wednesday, attached to 40a Castle Street, to advertise the local election the following day. The banner was very successful, motorists driving along the busy Gascogne Way could clearly see it.

Another important task for Monday was to complete the County Councillor role description. Hopefully this will provide enough information to encourage local people to stand as Independent Candidates.

The community newsletter is planned to go out at the end of the month. I spent the last hours of the day, researching local issues and events for Bengeo. Unfortunately there was not much material for media, so I emailed local people, including a leader of a meditation group and a local resident that recently completed a marathon for charity.

By the close of Monday, both me and Laura were very excited about the upcoming election and hoped that all are hard work would not be for nothing!

Wednesday

By Wednesday things were looking up for East Herts People. We all were very excited about the election on Thursday and spent a lot of the day preparing for election day. I again spent some time on Wednesday, working on community newsletters, which finding the relevant information was proving to be difficult.

Thursday – Election Day

8.00-8.30

Thursday was an extremely busy day, we all started early at 8.00am. Our first task was to attach posters and the loudhailer to Jim's car. We then all headed to Castle Hall to see the first polling station. At this moment in time there were few voters and left Laura here to be a teller for the next area.

8.30-10.00am

I was then whizzed off to the Sele Farm polling station to perform 'telling'. Telling is the electoral process of party (or non-party!) volunteers collecting electoral role numbers from voters. Telling enables the party/candidate to have a rough estimate of turnout on polling day. Unfortunately due to electoral legislation, Tellers must not be political active outside the polling station and are only able to show their political allegiance by wearing a rosette. Armed with a rosette and a chair, I sat outside the polling station asking for voters polling numbers. Unfortunately polling day was cold and I found myself shivering outside the polling station! I stayed at this polling station for around an hour and found telling at this station a mixed success. The voter turnout was very low, in an hour only around 20 votes turned up. But on a positive note, nobody refused to give me their polling number and in general voters were extremely friendly.

10.00-10.45am

I spent the next forty five minutes handing out Jim's campaign leaflet to members of the public in Sele Farm shops with Laura. Some people were very friendly and took leaflets, while some were quite rude and refused, this included a current Conservative Town Councillor!

10.45am -12.45pm

From Sele Farm Jim drove me to the Morgans Walk polling station at Morgans Primary School, where I again performed some telling. The voter turnout here was very low, but people were very friendly. I found that the majority of voters at this polling station were elderly, but were all very friendly and many engaged in conversation with me. It was very sunny at this point, and it was quite nice sunbathing and getting a little bit of a tan!

12.45-2.30pm

Jim drove me into Hertford Town Centre to talk to local people and to give out election leaflets with James. After this, I did feel like I had no dignity left! I spoke to many passers by and asked who they voted for and my general line was to hand out a leaflet to an individual stating 'vote Jim Thornton'. It was a mixed success, some people took leaflets and spoke to me about Jim and East Herts People and some simply ignored me.

2.30-4.00pm

Break

4.00pm-5.00pm

Jim drove me around Hertford Town centre and the suburbs and I used the loudhailer to encourage people to get out and vote. The whole experiencing was quite embarrassing, many kids found it very amusing, but it was still good fun! I found the best message to use on the loudhailer was 'Vote Jim Thornton' and 'Fed up of politicians and political parties, then vote for the independent alternative, vote Jim Thornton'. I am not sure how effective using the loudhailer was as there were not many people in their gardens or on the streets.

5.00-5.30pm

Myself and Jim dropped by at some of the smaller polling stations such as The White Horse in Hertingfordbury and the Hornsmill Community Centre. We spoke to the staff at the polling stations who seemed thoroughly bored as voter turnout was very low!

5.30-7.00pm

Myself, Jim, James and Laura headed to Hertford North to give out leaflets to commuters coming back from work. We also had a banner which we took turns to hold. The banner displayed information on Jim and the polling stations. The banner was excellent as motorists driving past Hertford North were able to read it and pedestrians walking past could also read the message.

Around 6.00pm Jim and Laura went to Hertford East. Myself and James took it in turns to hand out leaflets and to hold the banner.

Handing out leaflets was not very successful. Many commuters were not very receptive and most did not accept leaflets.

7.00-10.00pm

I finished the day telling outside Sele School. Between 7 and 9 it was very busy and there were around 80 voters an hour. Many were very friendly and no-one was hostile towards me.

After 9 only a handful of people came to vote. I was kept occupied by the school cat who decided to use me as a cushion!

Just before 10.00pm Jim came and picked me up and we went to see the sealing of the boxes at the polling station at Castle Hall.

10.00-11.30pm

All four of us then drove to Ware to nervously wait for the verification. The relevant boxes for our ward arrived at around 10.45. The polling staff opened some of the boxes and separated the votes into piles of European and County Council slips. Even though the votes were not being counted, we could see the markings of the slips and this gave us an idea of who may win.

We only saw two boxes being opened that evening, but we immediately knew that we had not won. Peter Ruffles had an enormous amount of slips, and even though we were disappointed, we hoped that we could still come a close second. We called it a night at half eleven and eagerly awaited tomorrow for the actual count.

Friday

10.15am

I met Jim at his house and we drove to Woodson Park, where the count was taking place. We met James and Laura there.

When we got to the count the verification had taken longer than expected and the count would not start till eleven. We waited in the lobby biting our nails.

11.00am -1.00pm

At eleven they started counting. All of us oversaw the vote and checked that all votes were being properly checked and counted. It was clear from the start that Peter Ruffles have won outright, we hoped that we would come a close second.

Around 12.30pm, Laura was called over as Jim's Agent to discuss the final result. Jim Thornton had came a respectable second, getting double the votes of both Labour and Lib Dem candidates. Whilst it was excellent that we came second it was highly disappointing for all of us. We all put in so much effort, more than any other party, it was hugely depressing that we came second.

Peter Ruffles (Conservative)	2,253	(56% +5%)
Jim Thornton (Independent)	831	(20.70%)
Tony Bodley (Labour)	499	(12.40% -14%)
Sean Shaw (Lib Dem)	416	(10.3% -5%)

Poll: 38.9% , total electorate 10,350
Average turnout across the County 39.3%

12.30-4pm

Myself, James and Laura headed to Ware for a Thai lunch to commiserate and celebrate coming second. We were all very disappointed but proud of the effort we put in. After the lunch we went home for a well deserved sleep.

7th June- 29th June 2009

It was hard to not feel disappointed that we lost the Local County Council elections in June. Even though we may have come second, there really is no place for runner ups in politics. After all our hard work, I admittedly felt sad, but was glad that over 800 people had voted for us.

8th-12th June 2009

One of the main tasks was to prepare a database of contacts for each of the Wards in Hertford that could be used to gather information for the local community newsletter. This turned out to be quite a task! It took me several days to finish up the database with Laura and James, but once it was completed, we had hundreds of contacts which would enable us to put together an informative community newsletter for each ward.

During this week, there was lots of media interest on the rise of the BNP. As a result of this, I wrote a blog entry on the BNP, which received a comment (that showed that people were actually reading our website!). I also updated twitter regularly with new photos and new mini blogs.

15th-19th June 2009

During this week I spend much time preparing the Guide to Being a County Councillor. Even though this may not be useful now, since we just had county election, it will be useful in future elections/by-elections and local people's understanding of what a County Councillor does.

I also wrote another blog entry on the closure of the Hertford Marquee Club and did usual job duties, such as media monitoring, updating Twitter/Facebook

22nd-26th July

This week was unusual since I worked 4 days (Mon, Wed, Thu, Fri) instead of 3 days a week (2 days a week at Save the Children) it was nice to spend some more time with the EHP team! This week was dominated by finding candidates for the community newsletter.

At first we were finding it hard to find information for the community newsletter, no-one wanted to be associated with a political party. As soon as Jim made the decision that the community newsletter would be separate from EHP, the emails flooded in. There obviously was a need for a community newsletter in Hertford. I spent a whole day ringing up companies and local organizations, and many we're willing to give us information, as long as we didn't mention EHP!

I also spent most of Wednesday preparing for the presentation on Independents to a sixth-form politics class at Davenant School in Loughton, Essex. We divided the tasks between us and I was responsible for discussing the arguments for Independents, current Independent politicians and councillors in the UK and also our election campaign. We created a PowerPoint presentation to assist us in our talks.

On Thursday we met at the office and drove to the school for the talk to be given at 10am. The talk went very well. I was extremely nervous at first, during the first two minutes I felt my heart racing! But I soon calmed down and was able to give a good talk, James and Laura were excellent too.

The 6 formers were great as well, they asked us questions at the end and debated with us why young people we're not involved with local government. We left them with written information on how they can be actively involved with local politics and I greatly hope some of them will get involved, as they were a bright bunch.

I really enjoyed talking to the students and wished that we were able to talk to some more school students. It was a great way to engage with young people and also highlighted the problem that Politics A-Level focuses on central government, leaving young people unaware of the structure and importance of local government.

We returned back to the office around half eleven and due to the recent political scandals revolving around Hertford Town Council I wrote an article entitled 'Hertford Town Council- Problems with Councillors and Transparency' and uploaded it to the website.

Some of the article concerned John Hedley who evidently didn't like the contents of the article and sent us an abusive email on the following

Monday. This evidently proved that the rumors surrounding Cllr Hedley's conduct, especially his abusive behavior, was true. I also spent part of the afternoon, packing the office up along with James.

Friday was quite a sad day, as I spent most of the day packing up the office, as a result of the move. I was very sad that my time at East Herts People was coming to an end!

Monday 29th July 2009

Due to the move, I was unable to access a computer until 11.30 so spent the morning doing some general admin. After I gained access to the computer network, I wrote an article and blog entry on the local Hertford by-election. I was very surprised that only the Tories and us put forward candidates for the by-election. Especially since the East Herts Labour website, contains the July newsletter which stated that they were fielding two candidates for the by-election. The deadline for nominations was very badly advertised by the Hertford Town Council and we wonder if Labour didn't hand in their nomination papers in time. We raise the question in Twitter, but so far we have had no response.

Embarrassing Stories from my time at East Herts People

Mitre Court

This is possibly my most embarrassing moment ever at East Herts People. One Monday morning the whole office was experiencing severe technical problems. The internet and phone lines went down and me and Laura were left twiddling our thumbs. We decided to make the most out of the situation and deliver Jim's campaign leaflet in town.

I soon delivered many leaflets to homes in Hertford town centre that I previously did not realise even existed. After an hour I went to deliver leaflets in Mitre Court. I found a gate open at the front and strolled into Mitre Court. Mitre Court is residential housing for elderly people and is more like a fortress than an estate! I attempted to deliver leaflets around the estate, but was unable to gain access to many of the blocks of flats.

I soon discovered that I could not get out of Mitre Court, all exits were locked and as I was not a resident I did not have a key.

To make matters worse, I had left my mobile phone at the office and could not tell Laura or Jim that I was literally locked in to Mitre Court. Mitre Court was also completely deserted, the only resident I spoke to did not know any English! After an hour and a half of wandering around the estate aimlessly I started to get rather worried, I hadn't seen any residents who could let me out, so I started to think that the best thing to do would be to jump over the fence! Luckily I did contact a resident, by ringing a door bell, who let me out through the front gate.

Who thought that delivering could be such a nightmare? I feel sorry for the postmen and postwomen that have to deliver to Mitre Court. I am sure that I will not be the last person to get locked into the complex!

Election Day (Jim's Campaign)

During election campaigns I seem to spend most of the time losing my dignity! Jim's campaign was especially challenging! During the day we encouraged the public to vote by handing out leaflets in town, the stations and driving around Hertford using the Loudhailer.

Loudhailer- Drove around Hertford in Jim's car encouraging people to vote using the Loudhailer. Many people seemed amused by the Loudhailer and teenagers found it hilarious; it attracting quite a lot of abuse and we were subject to several rather rude comments! I found using a loudhailer quite daunting as I was aware that if I muddled my words everyone in the surrounding area would hear! On a scale of 1-10, I would give the loudhailer 8 for cringe factor.

Handing out Leaflets in Hertford Town Centre and Sele Shops- All 3 researchers also handed out leaflets during Election Day for Jim. I spent a couple of hours in Hertford Town Centre on Maidenhead Street handing out leaflets to passers by and also encouraging people to vote by chanting 'Vote Jim Thornton for Hertford St Andrews'. Unsurprisingly I found the whole experience very embarrassing, especially because I kept bumping into friends and acquaintances! I also handed out leaflets to several existing councillors, including Cllr Tindale and the current Mayor of Hertford, who were far from amused.

Distributing leaflets in Hertford Town Centre- During my time at East Herts People, I handed out East Herts People leaflets and postcards in Hertford Town Centre. I usually wore an East Herts People t-shirt or my normal clothes. This was again quite embarrassing as I regularly bumped into friends/acquaintances and several current councillors.

East Herts People Evaluation

The last few months have been a huge experiment and we have tried many different ways of engaging with the electorate. Whilst some of our methods have been very effective, other methods/tasks have proven to be very ineffective.

Successes:

Twitter- Twitter was a very effective method of gaining supporters and spreading our message. As a micro-blog we were able to publicise and post links to our website. It was also a great way of finding out about new internet phenomenon's, such as the anti-BNP 'Hope not hate' online petition by the anti-fascist organisation Searchlight. I also used the site to raise debates on local issues and start conversations with young people on politics.

I think that Twitter was very successful as we had something to offer users who may not necessarily be interested in politics. For instance, we 'tweeted' on a wide range of subjects from reporting local news to giving interesting facts on Hertford. I don't think we would have so many followers if we only tweeted on independents.

Schools- On the 25th June 2009 all 3 of us went to Davenant School in Loughton, Essex and gave a 45min presentation to 6-form politics students on local government. I really enjoyed talking to students and I hope that we gave an inspiring talk which would encourage the young students to get involved with local politics.

Even though I categorised this as a success, it could also be viewed as a failure, since we only gave a single talk to a single school. In March I sent letters to local schools, explaining who were and stating that we could give free presentations on local government. At first the politics teacher at Simon Balle contacted us and Laura and James went to meet him in person. But he soon lost interest and we never gave a talk in Simon Balle and we never found out why. I feel this may have been because they were suspicious of our motives and didn't see us as a reputable political party.

Postcard- The EHP postcard (created in March) proved to be extremely useful. It was aesthetically pleasing and I loved the design. It explained briefly who we were and where people could find out more about us. We were able to leave it in shops and local businesses and also use it to accompany correspondence.

Jim Thornton's Election Blog- I thought this was an excellent idea and it got quite a following. Jim's blog entries were always entertaining and discussed the unglamorous side of running an election campaign. It also included amusing stories, such as Jim being bitten by a dog after delivering a leaflet! Poor Jim!

County Council Election-It was hard to not feel disappointed that we were the runner-up in the election and I felt desperately bad for Jim. But in hindsight it was actually positive that we came second.

We advocated individuals voting for a person and not the party and that is exactly what happened. The electorate voted for Peter Ruffles because of who he is, not because he is a member of the Conservative party. I met one of my brothers friends during election day, who told me he voted for Peter Ruffles because he was a nice guy and I couldn't argue with that. Peter Ruffles was known and loved by everyone in Hertford, we lost because of his popularity.

It was fantastic that we came second and also surprising. It showed that the people of Hertford thought we were reputable and 831 supported Independents. I am a firm believer that if we stood against anyone apart from Peter Ruffles, undoubtedly we would have won!

Website- In a few months we were able to set up a successful website that had regularly visitors. At first I was unsure of the merits of having a blog, but by the end saw it as an effective way of communicating a mixture of local news and events and thoughts. It was also a great way to keep our supporters updated with what we had been up to.

I really liked the issues section of our website, as it always contained interesting articles on a wide range of subjects, I hope this continues in the future,

Jim Thornton Campaign's Leaflet- This undoubtedly was the best campaign leaflet by any candidate. I thought it was honest and gave a good explanation of Jim's character and what he would do if elected. I thought it was an extremely professional leaflet and much praise to Simon for the design.

Failures

Facebook- We set up a Facebook group for EHP in March and it was a massive disappointment. At first we tried to keep it regularly updated, but it was soon apparent that it was not working. We only had a handful of people following us and most of them were our friends! We only rarely updated later on as it was simply a waste of time.

I think the reason that Facebook was so unsuccessful was not because Facebook is losing popularity (it currently has millions of users) but because you need supporters active on the site before you begin. For instance unless people had heard of us, it was unlikely that they would search for our Facebook page. Basically Facebook was terrible at recruiting supporters and that is the main reason it was unsuccessful.

Handing Out Leaflets in the Town Centre- We thought it would be a good idea to hand out our leaflets in the town centre for two reasons. Firstly because it would raise our public profile and secondly because we had many leaflets left over we needed to get rid of. The problem with handing out leaflets was that you had to obtain a license from East Herts Council, which was a pain. Also many people in Hertford did not accept leaflets from us, some because they already had them! We also had the problem that we were handing out leaflets to 6-formers who couldn't vote and also to visitors of Hertford. Unfortunately I feel that handing out leaflets in the town centre was a bit of a waste of time.

Hertford.net- When we first started researching Hertford websites, we came across the Discover Hertford Forum. The Discover Forum looked fantastic at first with over 1000 members. We soon joined at started commenting to topics and starting discussions. But unfortunately even though it had over a thousand members, only a few were active and they were not very receptive to us. Some members of the Hertford.net forum were quite aggressive towards us and one member started a conspiracy theory on us!

Advertising for Independent Candidates- As the Hertford by-election approached, we started to panic as we had no candidates for the two vacant seats on Hertford Town Council. As a result of this we put a small advert in the Hertfordshire Mercury.

Unfortunately we hardly had any responses and as a result I don't think it is a good method of recruiting candidates.

The Future of East Herts People

East Herts People has real potential to become an influential organisation for Independent politicians across East Herts.

We have achieved so much in the last few months and we have shown that the people of Hertford are willing to explore Independents in Local Government, but we must keep the momentum going. For us to succeed in the local elections in 2011 we must keep active.

I suggest the following actions between now and the next election in 2011:

- EHP should remain active and sustain a public presence.
- The website is updated regularly with articles and blog entries on local issues and local government.
- Our Twitter page is continued and regularly updated.
- In the future it would be beneficial to explore engaging with young people using Youtube and Podcasts.

- We should contact other Independent organisations and Resident Association political parties in the UK
- We should maintain a public presence by attending local events and market stalls.
- EHP should continue reporting on local issues but should remain unbiased, no matter how controversial the topic. We must maintain that we are Independent.
- We should continue to use our website and twitter page to campaign against the ruling party.
- We should continue to campaign against voter apathy and encourage young people to become politically active.
- We should continue to do leaflet drops
- We should continue to send e-newsletters to supporters.
- We need to recruit volunteers and supporters to enable EHP longevity
- We should bring back paid membership to EHP

Below is an explanation for each action. I believe that for EHP to thrive in the future it is essential that the website and social media sites are maintained at all times.

Technology

A huge question looms over current politicians, how do you communicate with the public? How do you maintain a public presence? Whilst in the past this would have been by regular canvassing and going to local events, these methods are no longer adequate. The postmodern society we live in demands that everything moves very fast; the challenge to the politician is to try and keep up.

Previously politicians would communicate with their electorate by 'just being out and about in a community' but this is no longer an effective method. Since many of us live in large Suburban towns, ambling around a community will only lead you to come into contact with a small percentage of the electorate and this is likely to exclude the younger generation.

We recently interviewed Cllr Debbie LeMay, Independent Councillor for Buntingford, she stated that she maintained a public profile by strolling around Buntingford Town Centre. But how many young people would feel comfortable discussing politics to a stranger in their sixties? Not many.

Many politicians may rely on local media to communicate with the electorate, but this method should not be used independently. The main problem with local media is that they are not widely read, and young people especially are very unlikely to have read local papers. I had never read the Hertfordshire Mercury until I started working for East Herts People.

Technology has proven itself to be a powerful tool in local politics; our Twitter page has been extremely successful with over 150 people currently following us, which is well above the average user. After all three of us have left, it is essential that our Twitter page is regularly updated, if it is not we will lose our current followers.

We currently have an excellent website, one of the best political websites in Hertfordshire. Other local political websites for the main political parties are hardly updated, badly structured and old fashioned. Our website by contrast, is regularly updated with blogs and articles.

It has been fantastic that people have been leaving comments on our website and discussing articles with us face-to-face. For instance on Election Day it was great to hear current Councillors' views on our website, even if some of them were slightly negative! It shows that our website was read by a large number of people and encouraged debate.

Like our Twitter page it is extremely important that our website is maintained after we leave. We do not want it to become like another opposition website, which is redundant, and outdated. It makes us look inactive and damages our reputation. It is a mistake for any opposition party to suddenly burst into activity only during elections.

Voter apathy among young people deeply worries me and the best way to combat it is to communicate with younger people using mediums they use all the time and of course we all know that young people love technology. If East Herts People really wants to engage with young people we must explore and maintain new ways of communication.

As stated earlier, we must regularly update Facebook, Twitter and our website and also look at other ways of communication. In the future it would be fantastic to explore producing videos that could be published on YouTube and podcasts that could be uploaded to our website.

Networking

Fringe political party are generally stereotyped as having extreme fanatical views and are hardly taken seriously. To combat this we must network with other organisations that would improve our reputation and we also must increase our public presence.

Firstly we should contact local organisations that support Independents across the UK. When I started here at East Herts People I had hardly ever head of Independents before and I believed that our organisation was one of a kind. But research undertaken by us has shown that we are actually nothing special. There are dozens of Independent Alliances/groups across the UK, along with Resident Associations that have evolved into small local political parties. Contacting these groups would allow us to swap notes and gain tips on ways to be a successful Independent organisation.

To enable East Herts People to improve our reputation, it would be very beneficial for EHP to be active in local events. The local Labour party had a stall in a recent community day in Hertford Castle and there is no reason why we cannot do the same. We also should have more market stalls at the weekend, as this increases our public presence. Just by being 'out and about in the community' we will hopefully be able to speak to local people who may become supporters in the community.

Campaigns

I think it is extremely important that EHP does not align itself to any particular viewpoint or local issue, as we are supposed to have no political viewpoint or belief. For instance the local Labour activist, Tony Bodley, campaigned strongly on Archers Spring in Sele Farm. Archers Spring is an area of greenbelt land in Sele Farm that was being misused by motorcyclists, as they had formed ramps and a dirt track. The motorcyclists in Archers Spring not only damaged the land, but also had a detrimental effect on local residents, who had problems with noise and air pollution. If we did the same, we risk becoming seen as single-issue independents and contradicting ourselves that we have no political bias.

But this does not mean that we cannot provide information for Independent Councillors/candidates on local issues. For our website, I think it is vital that we have articles/blog entries on local issues, but we must keep these unbiased as much as possible.

An area which East Herts People can be seen to actively campaigning for in the future (since it is not aligned to any political spectrum) would be to increase voter turnout and encourage younger people to become actively involved with politics.

Leaflet Drops

Between elections it is essential that in the future we maintain leaflet drops. Leaflet drops are expensive, so therefore we should distribute them as often as financially possible, a suggestion would be every six months.

I do believe that leaflet drops are important as it is an effective way of promoting ourselves. Whilst we may have contact with a few hundred people on our website and through Twitter, this is only a small percentage of the electorate. The negative side of leaflet drops is that many may go straight in the bin, but at least it allows us to contact people who have never seen our website, do not follow us in Facebook and do not have access to the internet.

As an opposition party

The County elections in June and the upcoming Hertford Town Council by-election have shown that we are the main opposition party. Local Labour and Lib Dems put together a very inefficient campaign. It was not surprising that we came second in June and that only the Conservatives have put forward candidates for the by-election in July. Since we are the direct opposition to the Conservatives, we must make sure that we are one step ahead at all times. Therefore East Herts People must ensure that we are active in-between elections.

There is nothing worse than the opposition party simply popping up just before an election, it does not fool voters. Our website is a fantastic opportunity for campaigning against the Conservatives and as mentioned before, it must be maintained at all times. It is a great method of communicating with the electorate the benefits of Independents whilst at the same time showing the Conservatives as incompetent.

The Twitter page has also been great at advocating with the public the benefits of Independents. Again our Twitter page should be used at all times to highlight the current administration's problems.

Currently East Herts People has little or no supporters. We desperately need to recruit volunteers to help with the running of East Herts People, as it is currently not financially viable and cannot simply run on paid employees, it needs public support. In my opinion I think we should bring back paid membership, even if it is a very small amount. This will allow members of the public to engage with our work and also let us know who supporters are.

Newsletters

I wasn't directly involved with newsletters myself, as this was James' responsibility, but these were a great way of keeping our supporters updated on our work. They were very cheap too, as these electronic newsletters were sent by email. The newsletters were very quick to put together and I see no reason why they shouldn't carry on in the future.

Appendix 4
James's Diary

James Turrell read History and Politics at Warwick University, and worked as an Intern with a Lib Dem MP in the House of Commons in 2008. He worked part-time for East Herts People from March to July 2009.

February '09

Researching the role of independent politicians in Canadian national politics; there's a long history of them in the Canadian Commons. One thing that struck me from a TV interview with one of the Independent candidates for the 2008 federal elections was that he had little to say except for the fact that he's not part of an apparently 'broken party system'. Cue rhetoric about standing up to the faceless party machines that quell things like 'genuine debate' and 'real opinions'. Described himself as a 'jack of all trades' who has branched into politics; more like stumbled. There is a real risk of coming across as casual politician, running only on the novelty of not being tied to a party, with no policy answers and nothing for people to identify with.

On researching UK independents, it seems they are most successful in local governments where the Tories are weak; they often form into cluster groups e.g. 'residents associations' to provide a united bloc within the council. It is common for them to have formed in response to a single issue e.g. council tax/hospital closed. The best example of a high-profile independent in the UK was Martin Bell MP, who overturned a safe Tory seat with the cooperation (abstention) of Labour and the Libs. His campaign was sparked and fuelled by a sleaze scandal involving the Tory incumbent and a feeling of public resentment towards mainstream politicians.

Having searched for material on independents it is clear that quality sources are pretty scarce and scattered/outdated where available. It suggests to me that many find keeping the ball rolling a difficulty; perhaps due to a lack of resources/money/the seasonal nature of electoral politics? This seems to be a problem with local politics in general, as many local people will only hear from their representatives or candidates when it is to secure their vote. I can understand why people may feel cynical about local politicians when they only go to the electorate out of cynical self-interest.

As for the website, the main issue with the current one is that it looks old and lifeless. We need something with more user interaction that can be easily updated by the researchers. People who see this may be instantly turned off. Looks like faded toothpaste packaging. We can't expect people to visit it regularly unless it is updated regularly and provides a service relevant to them; perhaps providing local issues and elections coverage in a single place.

Looking at new media and the Obama campaign, you get the feeling that he won because he was the popular candidate with all the new media toys rather than one who became popular through the use of them. It helped greatly that the type of people likely to vote for a candidate like Obama are the most technology-literate. Huge proliferation in broadband use among black Americans helped too. He had a huge network of volunteers working in localised cells. Nonetheless, I think the victory had more to do with George Bush than Facebook. People see through most electioneering, so they're only receptive when it sits well with them in the first place.

March 2009

Working form home – coordination of tasks with other guys difficult. Esp. in leaflet design – often seem to be covering the same thing.

Writing material for first leaflet release: the main problem is explaining to people how a party for independents works, since the concept of party contradicts the whole point of non-alignment. Things would be easier if EHP didn't have to carry the 'party' tag e.g. 'an organisation that supports people who don't belong to a party' rather than 'we are a party for people who don't want to belong to a party'. Obviously the party status is necessary for practical purposes but it doesn't lend well to succinct literature.

We've had trouble with content for the first release: squaring the message that people should vote, irrespective of who for, with the message that you should vote independent is difficult, especially within the confines of just one leaflet. Perhaps we need more than one? The risk is that we are convoluting our message and identity; one that is already quite tough for people to get their heads around. I am worried that an apparently neutral message will come across as underhand to people as they will have no trouble seeing through it. Most other independents seem to hammer home the 'not tied to a party' message without spreading themselves thin.

We received the new website design from Simon. It is exactly the thing we were looking for, looking fresh and modern. Now needs the back office to make it easily updatable and manageable.

Looking into social networking to get our message across, it seems that it is only likely to work well if people know about us already. We can't realistically expect many followers until we've sent leaflets out with our address on it, as people simply have no way of knowing we exist even. The fact that we can't invite people en masse to join our Facebook group is very limiting.

You can do this on Myspace but relatively few kids use it anymore and its set up to cater for bands, not organisations. I see people's use of social networking sites as an extension of their private space; most don't want this invaded by a group spouting about politics, no matter how prettily we package it. Sites like MySpace are essentially about music and fashion; to crowbar political issues into such an apolitical environment will appear patronising and gauche.

New website up and running courtesy of Nick – simple to upload content and appears as rolling news feed, easy to update regularly and keep fresh. We're not yet sure of how to approach users' comments. We want people to use the site to express views but need to moderate what they actually say; for now we're not expecting many visitors so comments appear automatically.

Once comments have started to come in we've realised that there's no compulsion for people to leave their email address when commenting, meaning we have to respond to them on the webpage rather than in a private email, which isn't ideal in all circumstances. Seems like very few people are commenting and we have a regular visitor who leaves snide one-liners on our articles. How incisive.

April 2009

We've been trying to find local issues that we can run as stories on the website, hoping that we can pull together a tidy source of all local news. It is a matter of scraping the barrel at the best of times. Starbucks' annexation of Bircherley Green and flattened gravestones are the biggest stories of the day.

They have been done to death by the Mercury anyway. The local press is near-on devoid of content with little of much consequence happening in Hertford to get people's attention. The Mercury might actually be hiring chimps to write stories. Apparently the local papers have been scaled down and centralised in recent years, though is this because people aren't interested in local issues and politics anymore? It's much safer to run human interest stories than make something out of the dreary intrigues of local government.

New leaflets and postcards – great! Delivering them about town gets a mixed response. Few people are openly hostile to us when we ask for a space in their shop window, but you get the impression they often agree to it just to get rid of you. I suppose this is understandable as workers have to put their neck out to display the leaflet, but not so for binning it once we're gone. Quite a few "don't do politics". As an exercise in selling EHP to people, we found it difficult explaining ourselves as an organisation without boring/scaring people to death. It was much easier to say "we're trying to get people to vote, can you help?" I was genuinely surprised by the number of people who agreed to take the leaflets. Shame nobody had them up the next day.

I set up the weekly email newsletter, intended to give subscribers a short summary of current issues and what EHP have been up to over the course of the week. The mailing list is only 6-strong at the moment, but the first release has had responses, with people asking who the EHP candidate in their division is going to be. Unfortunately at the moment we can't give out any specifics (except that there will be a candidate) which may be a problem. I get the impression that people lose enthusiasm once you turn them down on this. It kind of goes against our image as a proactive, happening party.

We've written to local businesses explaining ourselves and asking for support. We didn't expect much of a response and just one of them gets back to us; a man from a local printing works. He is angry about being snubbed by EHDC for printing their materials and says they've outsourced to Leicester. He maintains he isn't self-interested.

We've also been writing letters and commentary to the local press, who have been relatively receptive to us. The story run in the Mercury on EHP was twisted out of context (picking up on a passing comment critical of the Youth Town Council). The story successfully covered our voter and youth participation message, but the pushing of independents as an alternative to party councillors was weak. In fact it wasn't clear that we were there to promote independents.

Debbie Le May interview – she provided us with some useful insider knowledge for the press. Her story about us makes the Mercury (apparently desperate for material after the Easter bank holiday weekend!) but is spun as an attack on the youth council. A product of the loose message?

It turns out that the youth council have been so slow, as the person leading it died. This probably looks bad on our part, but Peter Ruffles assures us that people close to her understand the faux pas.

Seeing from Laura's efforts to introduce ourselves to Hertford's online community we tend to struggle with identity. People really don't get the concept of a party for independents. Many are overly sceptical; some think that EHP is working underhandedly, though perhaps because they are typical internet forum weirdos. Some are worried by the HSCPM link.

The fact that we can't say anything about Jim is a big problem as people want to know your policies and what you can actually do better than the party councillors. Until we can do this we are essentially toothless. Some don't see the point of EHP altogether. Positively though, the 'online community' consists of about 13 regular users, so this is by no means a good indication of sane people's opinions and very easy to blow up out of proportion.

We have been working on the community newsletters. Making individual ward editions is problematic as in some cases there's not really that much going on e.g. Sele – the community sports hall (run by Pam Grethe) refused to let us promote events there as they receive council funding. Most entertainment and events happen in the town centre. Kingsmead is especially difficult. The main issue I can see is that in being specific to each ward, you are potentially omitting important news and events because they are happening on the other side of an artificial divide. Perhaps a single newsletter edition with ward-specific news where possible would be more realistic?

May 2009

The official campaign period has begun so now we can tell people about Jim running as a candidate. I think this will help us clarify to people what we're actually about and rebut those who have been sceptical.

I had a letter published in the Mercury, notifying residents of their right to petition for a Town Council by-election where vacancies have arisen, in response to a previous article on the vacancy that implied that the position would simply be filled by the Council itself. However, we haven't had any responses from people wanting to stand as a direct result of the letter.

We've been phoning around local pubs to ask for permission for Jim to come in and chat to customers. They are generally accepting, though many think that their customers won't be responsive. This sounds reasonable enough to me, as the last thing people want on a night out is to talk local politics. A few balk at the prospect of being associated with anything political.

I've been following the Archers Spring illegal motorbiking story. This has shown up the first sign of activity from the Labour camp, with Tony Bodley sending round a petition to have the dirt mounds used by bikers flattened. However, the petition itself leaves a lot to be desired as it isn't at all clear what it is actually for (i.e. requires previous knowledge of the issue). It states simply SIGN THE ARCHER'S SPRING PETITION – what? Looks like their attempt to get an issue to rally around.

Earth mounds flattened at the end of the month – no mounds, no problem. Tony Bodley no longer has an issue.

Have been researching issues for the campaign – councillors' attendance – the main issue here is that there is no concise record of attendance. Other councils (though admittedly nowhere near all) have attendance record stats for individual councillors on their websites. With these, you can select a specific councillor and see their records over the last few years.

In the case of the County Council, I had to resort for tallying up the registers for a years worth of each meeting. Most seem to have a good record, and the one or two attending fewer than half are definitely in the minority. EHDC on the other hand publish their records of attendance like good councils. Nonetheless, the whole issue links in well with the Sacha Bright story and current furore surrounding MPs' expenses.

Allowances – it is possible to draw a direct line with Parliamentary expenses, but HCC and EHDC are essentially clean. All records are published and the expenses claimed are by and large ones incurred from travel to approved duties. It would be a great stretch to try and turn this into a scandal, though people don't tend the issue rationally so maybe it's worth a go.

A Story emerged in the local press at the end of the month 'exposing' the expenses of local councillors at District and County. However, it simply reports on the basic allowances of the councillors; the Mercury even admits in the article that the actual expenses claimed are only minor and mostly for travel.

Peter Ruffles gets a mention as EHDC's highest claimant, though this only amounts to £200 or so on transport costs. I doubt this kind of thing is going to stir up people's anger and even if it were to, it is probably far too late to make a big difference on the outcome of the election. This seems like too much of a non-issue to credibly make a big fuss about during the campaign.

Writing councillors' guide pack – it is hard to get to the real essence of what being a councillor involves (especially at town level). An email from Peter Ruffles explaining some of the non-official 'in state' duties demonstrates what this actually is. Obviously the duties as ascribed by the book are not the be all and end all of what a councillor does.

June 2009

Polling Day – telling – I tended to get a good response from people, if only as a friendly face; a couple make a point of the independent rosette, though most don't see it and some mistake it for another party. People seem to sympathise with you for sitting there all day. This probably scored us points for dedication, especially since none of the parties even bothered to show their faces. Only a few people blank you or get precious about giving their polling number.

Loudhailer – despite being fun, I'm not convinced of the positive effect that shouting people down in the street from a car has on your electoral prospects. Whenever I've seen this kind of thing done in the past I've thought it a nuisance, though it is a good way of getting your name out there quickly and cheaply. Electoral spamming. It's hard to gauge how much of what you're saying actually gets heard when you're driving past people. Longer statements tend to get lost by the time you've passed, so it's best to stick to shorter outbursts.

Thoughts on the 2009 Campaign

The EHP message

I think one of the hardest tasks we had was in explaining to people what EHP actually is without confusing them with the idea of a post-modern alternative to party politics. Many did not see the point of a party to represent independent candidates, especially in a place like Hertford where there is no strong independent presence. It is not as though we had a diverse bloc of candidates to pull together under our banner.

That said, this was a period when people were looking to alternatives to the mainstream parties. I think many warmed to us if only because we had nothing to do with the expenses-swilling main three.

As an outsider group in such an insular political area, it is incredibly hard to show people that you will be doing things any better or differently than the incumbents are. Anybody in politics can, and will, claim that they're here to bring the big break from the corrupt norm and 'clean up' the current situation. People have heard this a million times over and to do so may well come across as trite or patronising, so I'm sceptical as to how much currency the independent label actually holds. Yes, the novelty of a non-aligned candidate will draw some people in, but I think it still comes down to the quality of, and familiarity with, the individual candidate.

Another obstacle we faced came from the dual message that EHP was promoting in the first few months, leading up to the election campaign. I think the promotion of independents along with a neutral encouragement to vote convoluted our message a little, and certainly made explaining ourselves to people a tougher exercise. We skirted around this issue in our literature by producing the separate postcard and leaflet releases, but I can't help but feel that people may have been confused by the two faces shown. People expect politicians and parties to be self-interested creatures, so I don't think there would have been any harm in pushing the 'vote us' aspect a little harder.

Aiming for the youth vote

Although this was one of the initial goals set out, we eventually put efforts to appeal to younger people aside, in favour of more direct appeals to the electorate.

I don't think this was a bad thing at all, as the notion that politicians need to develop 'youth friendly' ways of delivering their message is glaringly flawed. If young people are going to understand and get involved in local politics it will be through the same channels and literature as everybody else. We were right to use new media channels to get our message across, but this was never going to be the key to getting younger people to listen.

Using the media to get our message across

This is an area we were quite successful in, as the coverage we received in the local press was far greater than I had anticipated (based on the quality of the press, rather than us!). We learned the hard way how fleeting comments can be spun out of proportion by journalists (though admittedly in doing so they seemed to give our story more of a point), but fortunately didn't suffer for it.

Appendix 5
Postscript

When we started the project in March 2009, it was part of the deal that the Researchers kept diaries that we hoped we could publish one day as a way of helping to encourage more people to get involved in local politics.

I did not read the diaries until a few weeks ago, and found them a fascinating account. I had to make a few changes to avoid legal action, but generally these are as the researchers wrote them as they went along the campaign trail.

Livia is now working four days a week for the Independent Network, and one day for East Herts People. I decided that I could best help IN by standing for Parliament, and so am standing as an Independent in Poplar & Limehouse.

We have a branch office right in the middle of this constituency, overlooking the Limehouse Basin, and for many years my father and grandfather had a joinery works in Brodlove Lane, Shadwell. It is probably the most diverse and interesting constituency in the country, with Canary Wharf, waterside studios, the whole spectrum of housing, the press at Wapping, and fascinating multi-cultural areas.

I will be facing two sitting MPs, Jim Fitzpatrick of Labour and George Galloway of Respect, and David Jones has joined me as Political Researcher to run the campaign out of our Limehouse office. He also is writing a diary, and I hope it makes as interesting reading as the diaries of Laura, Livia and James.